Best wishes

Lyana June Newkirk

# BACK
# HOME
# WITH RUTH

By

Lyana June Newkirk

*Illustrated*

VANTAGE PRESS

New York / Washington / Atlanta / Hollywood

FIRST EDITION

Published by Vantage Press, Inc.
516 West 34th Street, New York, New York 10001

Manufactured in the United States of America

Standard Book Number 533-01933-8

In appreciation of her great
love for Scottville, this book is
respectfully dedicated to:
Mrs. David Falconer

# Contents

# Introduction

THE SUN shone brightly and the residents of Scottville, Michigan, were enjoying a pleasant summer afternoon. Ruth Falconer, age ninety-seven, sat in the lawn chair which was on her front porch and smiled at the author. "Come in," she said, "come in. I will show you the secretary that my father made two years before I was born, which was quite some time ago. He was a cabinet maker, you know." She rose quickly from her chair and one of the garters that held up her stockings came loose. She turned her back to the author so that she could refasten it and remarked in a low voice, "If that happens many more times, I am afraid that I will have to resort to panty hose yet!"

The secretary stood majestically in her clean dining room. Ruth Falconer does all of her own cleaning, cooking, and other household chores. She goes to church every Sunday and belongs to the local "Friday Club," which is a ladies' club in the community. She still bakes her own delicious homemade pies. The author followed her into the living room and admired some wax fruit that stood in a bowl nearby. "Yes," Ruth mused, "My mother made that from molds before the Civil War, when she was still single." She moved the fruit to a shady spot on the table, then remarked, "I have a lot on my mind today. My eighty-six-year-old adopted sister had a stroke and is in a rest home. I would like to have her come and live with me so that I could take care of her. I have really thought about it and would do it, only I am afraid it might tie me down and I would not be able to go to my Friday Club. No, I think I am just too busy to take that on." We moved over to some chairs near her television set and sat down to talk about Scottville, her town.

Ruth Falconer has lived in Scottville for ninety-three years. She has, literally, grown up with the town. She knows more about its heartaches and joys, its happiness and sadness, its pulsing life than anyone else anywhere. Ruth has been very active in her day. She has taught school, acted on the school board, taught Sunday School, been a practical nurse, ran a boarding house for teachers and, as she puts it, "had my fingers dabbling in a lot of little odds and ends."

Ruth's beloved home town, Scottville, is located in the center of Mason County on the northwest side of lower Michigan and is situated upon the dividing line between Amber and Custer townships.[1] It is nine miles east of the city of Ludington, and is nestled along the banks of the Pére Marquette River. Scottville is centered around the intersection of two United States highways. U.S. 10 runs east and west through town and, along with north U.S. 31, it makes up the main intersection in the center of town.

The early history of Scottville, Michigan, dates back to frontier days, when the red man was the only inhabitant of this area, and it shows how man's knowledge and effort can develop and dominate natural resources. In compiling research material for this book, the author has found much to appreciate and can only say, "How pleasant! How truly pleasant it is to look back; back to frontier days!" In the search through books, records, and memories for material, the author has developed a feeling of kinship with all those who have struggled to make Scottville worthy of being part of the United States of America. Even though the change from frontier days until the present has progressed steadily, it has not been a rapid or "boomtown" type of expansion. It has taken time and the tireless effort of many people to create the development and prosperity of Scottville as it is today.

There is a twofold purpose for this book. First, the author

wishes it to create a picture of past events so that future generations will better understand and appreciate this tiny spot in America called Scottville which bore the slogan, "The Busiest Little City in Michigan." Secondly, the author not only wants to help the reader to know more about the history of Scottville but also wants to introduce him to Ruth, our warm, lively, lovely, ninety-seven-year-old friend. The reader himself may have passed this lady many times while she rocked on her front porch, and it might well be that her simple taste and the quiet colors of her clothes would not merit a glance from him. But if he came up and conversed with her, he could not ignore her. Her quiet serenity is captivating. From within these pages the reader may glean knowledge concerning the history of Scottville and become warmly acquainted with Ruth, Scottville's matriarch and leading lady.

The author wishes to acknowledge the contributions of all the people who gave so willingly of their time and vast knowledge of the area. A special thanks to Mrs. David Falconer, Mrs. Elva Reinoehl Deitz, A. O. Carlson, J. Ralph Reeds, Raymond Schulte, Mrs. Ruth Van Der Molen, George Crandall, O. J. Newkirk, George Mack, and the rest of the author's family. Also, a special thanks to the author's son, O. J. Newkirk, Junior, who allowed the author to glean from a manuscript he had written for a college history class. With so much enthusiastic help and inspiration from all of the above mentioned friends and family, the author has found the task of writing this book to be pleasant and very interesting.

# The Red Man's Twilight

THE INDIAN brave, dipping his paddle silently into the Père Marquette River, swiftly guided his bark canoe toward the right river bank. Before him was a steep timber-covered incline, and his gaze followed the narrow path which had been carved out of the mighty forest that covered the whole area. This snake-like path led between small openings in the tall and stately trees. He could see a crude dwelling of his tribe in each of the openings and smell the smoke from their fires as it lazily followed the air current down to the river. The evening meal was being prepared so it was time to pull his canoe up into the cool, tall grass and trudge up the narrow path to his own home. His squaw and papoose would be waiting for him. This was the red man's domain and stamping ground. Little did he realize that some day this area would become Scottville, Michigan—the agricultural center of Mason County, known as the "Busiest Little City in Michigan."

The Indians' main occupation was fishing and hunting, although they did raise some potatoes and corn. They did not have to work too hard to carry on their occupation. Bear and wolf were plentiful and there were numerous herds of the red deer within the wilds along the banks of the Père Marquette River. There were countless otter, lynx, mink, wildcat, and muskrat to make this area a model hunting ground. The Père

Marquette was full of choice fish; the air was full of edible birds; and wild berries grew in countless profusion. In fact, Mother Nature seemed to have emptied her cornucopia here for the red sons of the soil.[2]

The Ottawas who lived here were peaceful and often obtained some notions of civilized life from the white traders who came among them. In matters of dress, they tried to adopt the fashions of the whites, as far as the partially civilized Indian tastes would permit. It was not an uncommon sight to see the young Indian men fantastically arrayed in plug hats, black coats, and such of their native apparel as they deemed necessary to complete a gorgeous outfit.[3] Yes, the red man in the Scottville area was, indeed, happy and content with his way of life and his mode of living. The gods seemed truly pleased with him and were smiling down upon him.

In 1860, the cry, "Timber!," reached the ears of the red man. He stood with furrowed brow and listened to the sounds of advancing civilization. He shaded his eyes against the bright sun and watched as the tops of the most mighty and stately of trees swayed and smashed to the ground. He knew instinctively that he would have to find a new domain, further back, back away from his beloved Père Marquette River. And so they came. White men came with new hope. Here was land waiting for the ax and plow. Here was opportunity for anyone bold enough to take it. Out of such simple beginnings, a new community was born.

Before 1860, the red man had come in contact only with fur traders, hunters, and trappers. First there were the French, then the British, and finally the Americans. They were interested in gleaning profits from the fur trade and would give the red man blankets, spears, beads, firearms, and trinkets in exchange for the furs. The new type of white man that came among the Indians was not interested in furs alone. He wanted the trees which shaded the red man's brow and the soil from beneath the red man's moccasins. He pacified the Indians with treaties and small tracts or reservations on which the red man might continue to live. One small Indian village was located three miles southeast of Scottville near Custer, Michigan. It was nestled along the south banks of the Père Marquette River and forty rods west of the South Custer Road. Slowly the white newcomers displaced the Indian population of this area and the red man was forced to find a new home in or near the Indian village. Thus, the fur trade had declined and the days of lumber and agriculture took its place.

One summer evening, in the middle 1800s, an Indian brave guided his canoe downstream. He came from the Indian village, near Custer, and was on his way to Scottville. As the bow of his canoe cut silently through the water, he could hear the birds chirping in the trees along the banks of the river. The canoe rounded the river curve, near Scottville, and other sounds reached the brave's ears. From the north river bank came the sounds of the village, floating airily across the water. He listened intently. When he had lived there, the sounds that filled the air were of Indian drums and the chant of the squaws as they did their evening work. Now, the sounds that echoed forth were made by the white pioneers' saws, axes, and hammers. Yes, thought the Indian brave, how things have changed! How things have truly changed!

The red man turned his bronzed face toward the west. He saw the tiny slit of brilliant red which was all that was left of the setting sun as it slowly disappeared below the horizon. The Indian lifted his dark eyes skyward and noted the stillness of the leaves upon the mighty trees that still stood along the banks of the Père Marquette River. He allowed his eyes to roam down the rugged trunk of the beautiful oak that stood nearby and noted what a wondrous shadow it cast upon the still water of the river. Returning to his canoe, the red man slowly and silently started to paddle back upstream; back to his new domain at the Indian village. He paused for a moment and allowed the canoe to drift sideways while his eyes drank in the beautiful scene behind him. Raising himself, he stood straight as an arrow and raised his paddle high above his head in a final tribute and salute to his old stamping ground and domain. Then, settling himself down in the canoe, he paddled back upstream and disappeared silently around the bend of the river. In his heart, he knew that twilight had come for the day just passed, and also for him, the red man of the Scottville area.

# Timber-r-r-r

THE DEW was still on the grass and a misty haze hung in the still air. A new day was in the offing and suddenly the air was rent by a blast from the bugle horn, a large tin horn about six feet long used to rouse the boys in lumber camps and to call them in for meals. Voices responded to the call of the horn and suddenly men started pouring out of the log houses, or "men shanties" as they were called. The lumbermen would stumble down to the river or creek to wash for breakfast and then were ready to pack away the first meal of the day. They streamed over to the cook shanty, which was also built from huge logs. Each man swaggered in and tossed his hat to designate his "sittin' spot" on the long, log benches which ran parallel to huge tables that had already been set for the meal. Each logging camp usually contained from forty to sixty men and the cooks and cook's helpers were kept busy preparing food for the woodsmen. The men would line up and ladle their plates full of food from the "hashboard." Every once in awhile, the lumber camp would be blessed with having the camp foreman's daughter or the cook's younger sister as a "helper." It was very evident when a young, unattached, lonesome lumberman was interested in the kitchen help. His hair was always combed "wet-flat" and the top button on his shirt was always buttoned. He would throw his hat so that his "sittin' spot" would be closest to the kitchen and he could vent forth wise remarks and do other such worthwhile things for the sweet young thing's benefit. Everyone would fill their tin plates full of hashed potatoes, salt pork and beef, bread, fried cakes, cookies, dried apples, maple syrup, and grab large tin cups full of steaming hot coffee to wash it all down with[4] By the time the woodsmen had finished eating, daylight would be breaking in the east as long, slender shafts of sunlight streaked down through the tall and stately trees.

The first clearing and permanent settlement at Scottville began around 1860. Until then any clearing of the land had been done by the Indians. They were not interested in the freedom of the Negro population of the nation, nor were they interested in the presidential election of that year which gave the country a national leader by the name of Abraham Lincoln.[5] But there were white folks in the country who were extremely interested in national affairs at that time. Proof of this can be found by picking up a county map which bears such village and township names as Lincoln, Freesoil, Grant, Victory, Sheridan, and Sherman. Charles Mears, a prosperous county lumberman, donated pine boughs from Mason County to deck the platform at the Republican Convention which nominated Abraham Lincoln for the 1860 presidential election. Lincoln was sworn into office on March 4, 1861.[6] At this time currency throughout the whole country was still signed by hand. There were six employees in the United States Treasury Department who did this. During Civil War days, about forty Mason County men left for the army. This meant leaving their families behind to carry on alone in the dense forests.[7]

Louis C. Towns, who came to Mason County in 1863, described Scottville as being but forests with a few badly constructed cabins clustered here and there. Most of these were occupied by Indians. In 1863 there were only four white families in all of Amber Township. By 1864, the population of Mason County was 845 and this particular district, the future city of Scottville, had less than ten families.[8]

Logging in the early days was nothing more or less than "slashing." The choicest trees were taken, and no notice taken of any others.[9] The timber was largely beech, maple, hemlock, and elm. There was also a large quantity of pine timber. When cut, the timber averaged not less than fifty-five cords per acre. [10] The men who worked in the lumber camps were of all nationalities. Those who worked on the Père Marquette River, floating logs down to Lake Michigan, were mostly French-Canadians who had come down from Canada.[11] The region developed into a great lumbering center. An article taken from the *Western Monthly* magazine stated that 75,000,000 feet of lumber were cut in 1869 in Mason County alone.[12]

As was stated earlier, permanent clearings around Scottville began to appear in the 1860s when a few settlers came to work in the logging camps. Others came to homestead. At first, they chose pine land, since it was more plentiful and easier to handle, and settled near the river. Later on, they lumbered hardwood. Chicago was the coming market for shipping in western Michigan and sailing vessels were used almost entirely for this purpose. The logs from the lumber camps were floated down the Père Marquette River to Lake Michigan. At that time, there were a few sawmills being built in this locality, and Chauncey Record built the first blacksmith shop in Scottville.[13]

Due to the vast forests in the area, the lumber industry grew very rapidly. Transportation problems were really giving the logging companies something to think about. The only means of travel had been by foot, horseback, oxen, or by boat. In 1871 work was started on the east-west railroad from Saginaw to Ludington. The ties were laid and, much to everyone's joy, the train traveled directly through the area where Scottville would some day be located. After three years of hard work, the railroad was finally completed, and in 1874 Governor Bradley came over the line on a tour of inspection. As the train slowly coughed and chugged to a stop in the little community, Bradley stepped near the train door and raised his hat high in a salute to the occasion. The crowd of onlookers shouted and cheered in recognition of Bradley and also in glee over what had been accomplished. After all, Bradley was standing on the very first train ever to pass through the Scottville area.

The first train stop near the village was at a spot about a half mile west of Scottville at a little junction called Jordon. The clearance lay between Scottville and the community of Amber, which proved to be another stopping place for the train.[14] Every train that passed through Scottville filled the community with great awe and wonder. The small, unnamed village was just a flag station then, and when passengers wanted to board the train, they would take a lantern or lamp and swing it so that the engineer would know that he should stop there. Freight was thrown off to the side of the tracks, remaining there until the owners came for it. The engine of the train was fired with hardwood instead of coal. The fuel supply was replenished daily and certainly was no problem, with such vast areas of timber nearby. Thus, historically the railroad played an important part in both lumbering and agriculture in the area of Scottville, Michigan.[15] Before the days of the railroad, transportation and shipping to and from the village were very difficult. For many years, the only means was by a small tug that plied the Père Marquette River, bringing supplies which were unloaded and left on the river bank for several days and were seldom molested. These supplies were then carried in sacks on the backs of the men and occasionally the logging companies would send oxen for the heavier supplies.[16] The Père Marquette River was the only connection that the area had with the outside world. In fact, it was through this waterway connection that the pioneers of the community heard about John Wilkes Booth and President Lincoln's death.

After the trains came, Scottville began to grow very rapidly. Cordwood, waiting to be shipped out, could be seen piled high along the tracks at Amber, just west of Scottville. Lumber was stacked in large piles to season. When the piles reached a certain height, the lumber was loaded on large two-wheeled vehicles, pushed up long ramps, and piled up high, away from the trains. About once a week, a long string of flat cars arrived, were shunted to a side track, loaded with seasoned lumber, and shipped to all parts of the country.[17] This increasing activity around the train made it more and more apparent that the rail line, which stretched east to west across Mason County, was going to have quite an impact upon the growth and economy of the future city of Scottville, Michigan.

When the settlers first came to the Scottville area, they found it to be a mighty forest waiting for the great timber harvest. As the years passed, the ring of the axe, whine of the saw, and cry, "Timber-r-r-r!," finally gave way to the furrow of the plow, rails of the fence, and sounds of the barnyard.

—3—

# The Home Scene

THERE ARE times when every young boy or girl has negative feelings, even though ever so slight, toward their parents. Such was the case of a young teen-ager of pioneer days. The supper table had been cleared, dishes washed and put away, and the garbage from the kitchen had been dumped into the skimmed milk which was waiting for Papa to feed to the hogs as swill. Papa had carried the two swill pails out and sat them on the ground beside the back porch. It was twilight time and the oldest daughter felt that she should visit the outhouse or privy, as it was called, before complete darkness enveloped the area. She ran to the back door and, without looking down, took a flying leap over the side of the porch and landed with each foot planted squarely in a pail of swill. Negative feelings toward Papa surged within her as the swill ran down her arms and the potato peelings draped dramatically from her hair and shoulders. Many such humorous episodes happened during pioneer times and much laughter has pealed forth as the stories have been told and retold through the years.

The gradual influx of settlers in this area started to pick up momentum in 1865, when here and there, in the wide stretch of woods, farmers built little log houses with a few acres of cleared land around them and with winding roads or blazed paths through the forest as the only way of getting from one farm to another or from one settlement to another. The menfolk of the families worked at the various logging camps in the area and at times would only be home on weekends because the logging camps were situated even deeper into the forest, and the men would have to walk miles to get to them and walk miles to get home again.

The first main road to Scottville from Lincoln, then an active lumbering village, was blazed through south of where the railroad tracks now lie and was later to be known as First Street. This dirt road was used by many lumbering concerns to haul supplies from the lake village to their camps. No attempt was made to make a smooth road. It was just a trail that oxen, pulling a "toad", could travel over to bring needed supplies to the scattered settlers and to the lumbermen in camps. This narrow, angling, dirt road ran east and west and proved to be the only road from the Scottville area until 1875. The area where U.S. 31 and U.S. 10 would someday be located was considered beyond hope of clearing because of the abundance of swamps. The first north-south road came into being by late 1875. It led north to Manistee and northern Michigan and south across the Père Marquette River to southern Michigan. Five years later, the new road was surveyed and this gave the Scottville area an advantage over Custer and Amber, as it was a central point for the two roads.[18] Another point of great advantage for the area was the fact that it was located closer to the river than Custer and Amber. This gave it a closer tie, through transportation, with the outside world. Also, fishing was still very good in the area and the river was a popular place to catch tomorrow's supper. As Mrs. B. A. Schulte once stated: "The river was filled with fish. I caught so many suckers that my mother would throw them back into the river from our back door, but always kept the beautiful trout that I caught while wading in Sweetwater Creek. I used a homemade net to dip the trout from the water. Most of the early settlers are gone, but memories of those happy times linger on!"[19]

By 1870, a number of farms had been homesteaded in the central section of Mason County under the Homestead Act.

This law, passed by Congress, gave a quarter section (160) acres) of public land free to any man twenty-one years or older who was a citizen of the United States or to an alien if he had taken out his first papers. All the homesteader had to do to receive title to the land was to live on it for five years and show that he was improving it. Much land in central Mason County was homesteaded by farmers who claimed it under the Homestead Act.[20] The list of early settlers proved to be growing. Some of them were families of men who had been employed at the different lumber camps. They came and decided to stay. The Homestead Act helped the list of early settlers to grow even more rapidly. Some of the early pioneers in the settlement and the surrounding countryside were H. Judge who came in 1844, H. Quevilion in 1848, William Carter in 1860, C. W. Barclay in 1863, and Samuel Jensen in 1865. S. Warren, C. Record, Isaac Chinnery, and C. W. Jones were listed among the 1865-1868 comers. Warren Robinson, J. N. Mack, and Andrew Neil were listed in the 1871-1872 group. The homesteaders began to look for a closer place to trade rather than having to travel to Amber, Pentwater, or Lincoln near Lake Michigan. Mason Center, as it was called by many, became a favorite gathering and shopping spot for the folk in the surrounding area as well as for those who lived close to or in the little village.

In 1873, Harry Melson became the first white settler to homestead a large tract of land in Scottville and to receive his grant from the government. He built the first general store in the yet-to-be-named settlement. The structure nestled cozily between maple and oak trees on the east side of Main Street just two blocks south of the railroad tracks. The property, located at 403 South Main Street, was later owned for many years by Mr. and Mrs. E. K. Buckmaster. Being near the top of the Père Marquette River hill, Melson could get fresh water from the nearby springs and could carry water for the stock from the creeks. He was a good farmer and it was not long until he had a wagon on the trails, bringing groceries which he traded for butter and eggs. He made weekly visits throughout

13

the whole area and the children loved to see him coming down the path. In summer he traveled by horse and wagon and in winter he made his rounds with a horse and sleigh. One could hear the jingle of the sleigh bells as he came along through the white fluffy snow to trade supplies for produce, going from farm to farm. His wagon or sleigh was always filled with treasures and the children would climb inside to see what goodies were new on that trip. His load would be filled with the sort of things that all children like, such as the well-known stick of penny candy, a fancy ribbon, or a small ball. It also bore the more staple things for the older folks.[21] The pioneer women sometimes bought a pound of coffee, a few tomatoes, or a gallon of kerosene. They would, at times, trade a fat hen or some eggs for their purchase. Most of the activity in the area was north of the Père Marquette River, as there was no bridge over the river at that time. This made it very difficult to travel south of town. Before long, a crude log bridge was erected over the river at that point and Melson was able to extend his route to take in the area south of the Père Marquette River as well.

In 1873, the firm of Sweetland, Mustard, and Winters established a sawmill on the northwest side of the community, near the railroad tracks.[22] James Sweetland and J. C. Mustard arrived from Victory, where they had operated a mill. They, along with John Winters who had come to cut timber, established the new mill. The development of the mill was added evidence that the lumber industry had become a thriving business in the area. Sweetland operated the sawmill for a few years and then was hired by the government to establish a boardinghouse for the men who were road workers and were working on the new road being cut through to Baldwin. The boardinghouse was located in the southwest corner of the future main intersection in town.

Another first settler in the area was Andrew Falconer, Sr., a railroad engineer who came to the locality in the summer of 1873 from Glasgow, Scotland. His daughter-in-law in later years made the statement that, "Father Falconer did not know any more about farming when he came here than a bull knows about goin' to war!" Mrs. Falconer had been a dairy maid in Scotland, and she was more schooled in farming than in engineering. She had two brothers living in the area already and they were quite influential in getting the Falconers to come too. The trip to America was made in approximately two months and it took another six weeks by water to reach Grand Haven, Michigan. The rest of the trip to Mason County was made by ox cart.

Falconer brought his wife and young son, David, with him. At the time, David was only two years old. The wife thought that this seeming wilderness of woods was indeed a dismal place to bring her child. In fact, one of Mrs. Falconer's brothers finally went back to Scotland. He informed everyone that it was too difficult for him to stay in a place where there were so many Indians and where the country was so wild.

Falconer started to look for a place to make a home. He could have bought a whole quarter section within the area where the future city of Scottville would someday stand. The price for the quarter section would have amounted to six hundred dollars. He was known to have talked about this time and time again in later years. Mrs. Falconer would not consent to purchasing the quarter section. There were just too many Indians around the area. The Indians were still quite numerous northeast of the village and upstream along the Père Marquette River. She did not want to take a home which might entail neighbors such as that! The Falconer family settled on eighty acres just one half mile northeast of the village "as the crow flies." They built a four-room log house on the property and their second child, Jessie, was born there in 1874. During the next few years, three more children were born to the Falconer family.

Clearing the land of the beech, maple, and pine trees was job enough, but the pioneers also had to prepare it for cultivation. Besides doing the farm work, the early settlers had to also find a means of supporting their families. Falconer was no exception to the rule. He worked at a lumber mill at

Hamlin during the week, walking over ten miles home on Saturday night with his groceries in a grain sack flung on his back and leaving again on Sunday to return to the mill. He also helped to build the railroad to Ludington. The family developed the land into a fine producing farm and, eventually, young David Falconer sold and delivered milk to the villagers.

Not only the "grown-ups" were busy in those days. The children as well were kept busy and had plenty of chores to do. No one dared shirk and there certainly was no time to stand around and complain. If there were signs of rebellion among the children, father settled the whole affair in the woodshed before anyone had time to decide what was fair and what was not. Father was head of the household. He decided the matter for everyone and no one questioned his judgment because he demanded their respect and received it. There were no conveniences. All the water had to be carried from springs. Each one had to take a bucket and help tote his share. The boys helped in the woods, barns, and fields. They were expected to go to the woods and drag up long wood poles so that firewood could be chopped in different lengths. The wood was needed to feed both the cooking and heating stoves. The boys also became quite adept in handling a shovel and pitchfork.

While quite young, the children also learned the correct way to milk a cow. They were taught to sit on the cow's right side, place the end of the cow's switching tail in the bend of their knee, and brace their left leg against the cow's back leg. If this were not done just so, they could find themselves faced with the traumatic problem of figuring out how to get the cow's foot out of the half full bucket of milk. Also, they could experience the sting of the cow's tail as it lashed about and slapped the milker on the cheek, possibly leaving a brown stain, depending upon the cow's personal cleanliness. The younger generation also learned how to slop the hogs, husk the corn, and do the many menial odd jobs that were always found around pioneer homes.

The girls were found to be needed quite regularly to help

with the housework. There was baking and cooking to be done. The pioneers had chickens to fry and hams to bake. They "dressed out" their own hogs and hickory-smoked the hams. Butter was churned, and it proved to be very difficult in later years for folks to find buttermilk that tasted half as delicious as it did back on the pioneer farms. After the cooled wooden butter paddle had been used to remove the butter from the churn, each child was allowed to ladle out his own "tin-full" of sweet buttermilk. A dash of salt was added to it and it was slowly sipped, giving a feeling of complete contentment to the partaker.

Sunday was the time for company, and the day was a complete failure unless some friends or neighbors tramped through the woods and came to dinner. The womenfolk would kill a fat, plump hen and boil it in water until the meat was tender and ready to fall from the bones. Then, pot-pie was made and dropped in with the chicken into the steaming broth. A few cubes of potatoes were added and that, along with the vegetables, apple pies, huge sugar cookies, jugs of cold milk, and cups of steaming coffee made the meal a success. During the evening, everyone would sit down for friendly conversation and popped corn or maple syrup parties. Life was not cluttered with outside activities. All recreation of that time revolved around the home and family.

Herman Schulte, an experienced carpenter, arrived in the area in the 1870s also. Schulte built himself a nice home which stood where the 4-Star theatre would later stand. This had the distinction of being the first frame house to be constructed in the area. The earlier homes were all log houses. The structure was later moved to 107 East State Street and is still being used as a residence today. Schulte did a lot of the building and carpentry work in the area. He built the first boardwalks that were to rest upon Scottville soil. In later years, he helped build the first church, which was located at 201 East State Street. He also helped build many stores and the local schoolhouse.

The small children of the day long remember Herman

17

Schulte's wife. Their house, cozily tucked in amongst some large maple trees, had a white picket fence around it. Mrs. Schulte did her laundry out in the yard where summer breezes and the cool shade of the trees caressed her and lightened the tedious task. She was a very happy person with a beautiful voice and, much to the children's delight, sang lustily as she labored over the washtub. Schulte's son, B. A. Schulte, was the first white child born in the tiny settlement which eventually developed into the agricultural center of Mason County. The third and fourth generations of the Schulte family have also found Scottville to be a happy and pleasant place to live. By 1873, the little village was known as Sweetland, so named for one of the mill owners in the community; it was also called Mason Center by some folks because of its location. The abstract books in the area also listed it as Mason Center. The local residents of the tiny village all called it Sweetland. Some of the early residents who lived within the village in 1873 were the Harry Melson, H. Schulte, C. W. Jones, J. C. Mustard, James Sweetland, and John Winters families.[23] Within the next few years, or by 1880, George Reader, William Reader, Abraham Prindle, James Crowley, Hiram Scott, C. B. Clay, Mrs. Emma Bishop, Talcot Reader, and F. J. Reader had all arrived in the little village or surrounding countryside.

Thus the realities of the past were made by energetic pioneers who came here and formed the foundation for the agricultural center of Mason County — Scottville, our town!

# —4—

# The Village Scene

EVERY VILLAGE has a beginning or a time when its growth is quite pronounced and it appears that a town is blossoming forth. This also happened in the tiny community which was located in the center of Mason County. By late 1879, most of the business block of the village rested immediately south of the railroad tracks. Then things began to happen and the town began to change. It was not a period of fast growth; just steady progress.

In late 1879, Hiram Scott and James Crowley, lumber scalers from Ludington, joined their funds in a business venture and started a general store in a two-story building just south of the railroad tracks.[24] The two-story structure they moved into had been just recently built. In the December 12, 1879, issue of the *Mason County Record,* it was stated:

> Scott and Crowley have the frame up and the roof on for a store building at Sweetland's Station on the railroad, into which they will put a stock of general merchandise about the middle of the month. They will continue their business of buying bark, ties, logs, etc.[25]

Scott ran the store with Crowley as a silent partner and shortly after that time, they hired George Reader as clerk and assistant manager. They even served light lunches in one part

19

of the store. Reader and Scott were kept quite busy, for the mail and railroad sections of the establishment caused extra work in the general store and it took both of them to keep things running smoothly. While one was sorting mail, the other would be selling railroad tickets, and so on.

An amusing incident of those days concerns the way that one of these men as depot agent would take his station agent's cap off the peg and wear it to go out to meet the train. After the train had passed, he would then replace it with his more conventional hat or cap.[26] Even if the train was not going to stop, Scott or Reader would stand outside with their station agent's cap on and wait until the train had disappeared down the tracks. This cap made their job as agents appear much more "official."

In the early days, mail traveled by way of a route along the shore of Lake Michigan, coming from the south to Pentwater, then by boat or by horse to Ludington. The earliest settlers were obliged to walk the narrow paths and trails through the forest to Ludington if they wanted to receive their mail. By 1870, a post office had been established at Amber, two miles west of the future site of Scottville. At that time, Amber was more populated than the Scottville area. It possessed a mill, a store, and a physician. The Amber post office was conducted by Chauncey Richert, who later came to Scottville.

After Hiram Scott started his establishment, the mail for the village was dropped off there instead of at Amber. Scott and Reader had fixed up one corner of the store so that it vaguely resembled a post office. They placed two cracker barrels a reasonable distance apart and laid long planks over them. The planks were sectioned off by black paint and a local family name was placed in each section. The mail for each family was placed in the appropriate section. Thus, the first post office in the little village came into being.

With Reader taking over more of the management of the store, Scott found time to turn his attention to other interests. In late 1879, he build the first hotel in the village.[27] There was a succession of three managers in the hotel, and then it was partially destroyed by a fire of undetermined origin. It has been said that, while searching through the ruins, a skeleton of a man was found in the ashes. No one has ever been able to determine who the gentleman was who was lost in the fire. The part of the hotel which withstood the flames was later remodeled into a family home and was occupied by the Barton family until the early 1970s, when it was torn down. The building was located in the 100 block on the south side of First Street.

Also about a hundred years ago, Steve Darke built a building about one-half block south of the railroad tracks and conducted a meat market there. It was the first meat market in the community. As history shows, the late 1870s were really years of great change and growth in the Scottville area. In fact, the whole country appeared to be in the grace of prosperity. The great "Cattle Kingdom" or cattle boom flourished in the West during that same period in our national history.[28]

By the year 1880, W. A. Bailey was in the process of getting ready to build Bailey's Hardware Store. The building opened its doors to business at the corner of State and Main Streets. The next building to be erected was a village depot and it was followed by the construction of a restaurant by the Chinnery brothers. A Mr. Schriener built a whole block of buildings up from the railroad tracks. Part of this block contained the old opera house, which was later destroyed by fire. E. M. Briggs and F. J. Reader came to the area during the early 1880s and became most prominent in helping to build up the community.[29] They were instrumental in the building of many of the homes and stores in the area.

Life in the little community, even then, was not all sweetness and roses. There were stories concerning street fights, gambling riots, and conflicts with individual Indians. It all seemed to be just a part of pioneer life and lumbering days. It was at that time in the town's history that little six-year-old Katie Flynn had the whole area in a turmoil. She lived with her

21

mother and father just east of town and followed her father to work one bright summer morning. It was not long before word reached the village that she could not be found. Hunters and trappers joined the townfolk in a frantic search for her. After an exhausting two days and two nights of hunting for the little girl, she was finally found lying under a tree guarded by a great black bear that she called "Doggy."

Mrs. Mattie Clay, who lived just west of the village, came down to the kitchen one morning to get breakfast for her family and found Indians sitting at the kitchen table. Sometimes the Indians were peaceful and sometimes they made a lot of demands. After they had enjoyed the breakfast that she prepared for them, they left.

Mrs. William Carter, who lived just west of the village where the REA project was later built, was alone one day when a group of Indians came in and demanded food. Her husband had left for town to get flour, sugar, and other supplies which he carried on his back. When she could not give them food, one Indian squaw drew a knife from beneath her apron. Mrs. Salinda Carter stepped into her bedroom, reached for the gun that was hanging on the wall, and thus persuaded the Indians to leave. Pioneers long remembered the Indian calls, from one red man to another in the Fall of the year, to gather the Indians together for their annual Pow-wow.

In 1880 the first village jail was built near the railroad tracks just one block east of the main street. It was made of planks and was held together by spikes. William Tifts was a tinsmith and village constable. One of Tifts' greatest pleasures was to fire the anvil on the Fourth of July. He did it as a great feature of the day's celebration. Tift took his job as constable very seriously. He would make his rounds of the town with his badge glistening on his shirt pocket and his hat cocked back on his head. In his own way, he impressed children and adults alike with the importance of a constable in town. One night he arrested an inebriated lumberjack and placed him in the jail. The lumberjack's co-workers managed to help him escape and put Tifts' cow in the jail instead.

The village kept growing in spite of such incidents. Dr. Thomas arrived in 1882, and built a drugstore directly across the street from Scott's general store. Many are the stories of long and dangerous trips made in the early days and of the hardships that this good doctor endured. Many are the stories, also, concerning all of the buildings that were erected in our young and hopeful town during 1879-1882. Although most of the original buildings are long since gone, one could not wish them back for one would not want to stand in the way of progress.

# Ruth

IN THE beginning; beginning of him, beginning of her, God molded them and they were. So it was with baby Ruth Bishop.

Emma Bishop stretched out on the bed in her father-in-law's home and considered the unborn infant within her. She felt the pains gather force and shoot like lightning across her back and down her sides. Each time the pain visited her, it seemed to become more pronounced and could not be so easily shrugged off. After all, being thirty years old would more than likely make childbirth a little harder for her to master without difficulty. Finally, the day for her first-born to enter the world had arrived. October 23, 1876, was just beginning to blossom forth. The rays of the sun shot far up into the sky like long golden fingers trying to grasp the brilliant colors of the trees as their hues caressed the countryside.

Emma turned on her side and looked at Asa. In the sunlight of the early morning, she could see the strong lines of her husband's face as he peacefully slept beside her. They had waited a long time to have a baby. There had been so much work to do, so busy, always so busy. Four years had passed since their wedding day and they had worked hard to achieve success. Everyone in Ellisburg, New York, thought well of them. After all, he was a brilliant cabinet maker by trade and also helped on his father's farm. It was a large, fertile farm situated half in Oswego County and half in Jefferson County. Asa was also an ambitious church worker, and folks all around were always telling about how much he did for the church.

The pain stabbed again and Emma reached out to touch Asa, then changed her mind as the pain subsided. It was not yet unbearable and she decided to let him rest as long as possible. After all, their bed was going to be a very busy place before long and she thought he needed what rest he could get while there was still time. Emma gazed out the window at the brilliant red leaves of the maple tree and watched the shadows play tag on the colorful scene as her mind wandered again. She had done many things during the thirty years of her life, but this episode was surely different from any other that she had ever experienced. Emma was a graduate of the Old Union Academy of Belleville, New York, and had taught school most of her adult life. For the last few years she had been a practical nurse and had worked with a German doctor in the Ellisburg area. Both careers had proved worthwhile and exciting, but neither could match the career that she was embarking on at this moment — that of becoming a mother. The whole thing was absolutely breathtaking, full of awe and yet, full of pain also! Emma let a little moan escape her lips with the next flash of pain and reached hurriedly for Asa. The time had arrived.

After delivery, Doctor Reige gave the newborn babe a slap on the rump and a vigorous cry echoed throughout the chambers of the Bishop home. Everyone turned to ask the same question, "Boy or girl?" Doctor Reige turned the tiny being over and proudly straightened himself to make the grand announcement for all the world to hear. Little Ruth Bishop had entered the world.

The hot August sun penetrated the morning dew left by the coolness of the night and started again to bleach out the hard clay that made up the roadbed. Asa Bishop reached for his red handkerchief and mopped his brow. He was in a hurry. Asa wanted to avoid the heat of the day, and he was anxious to complete the cabinet that was half assembled in his workshop, but first the farm milk had to be taken care of and delivered to the dairy station. This was a chore that had to be done each and every morning, otherwise the milk might spoil. His father seemed to feel that Asa had more time than anyone else and had delegated that particular task for him to complete each morning when chores had been finished. Asa wished his father could better understand his great love of cabinetmaking. *There* was a task worth doing! He loaded the milk containers onto the farm wagon and hitched the team up to the whiffletree. Grabbing the reins with his left hand, he whirled their loose ends with his right and let them snap on the rump of one of the big geldings as he let out a loud, "Giddap." The horses seemed to sense the hurried mood that he was in and obliged by taking off at a fast pace. As the horses moved along, Asa settled back on the wagon seat.

Along the edge of the roadway, birds chattered busily and searched here and there for something to eat. They flew into the air with a noisy flutter of wings as the horses charged along and disrupted their search. Asa did not seem to notice. His mind was on his own little red-haired daughter. Ruth was just under a year old now. She was such a jolly, chubby little thing and a joy to both of her parents. Asa smiled to himself as he thought about her. He loved her so very much and she knew it. She could literally twist him right around her little finger. Wrapped in his thoughts, Asa did not slow down for the narrow plank bridge that had been placed over the deep gully ahead. The horses' hoofs clattered loudly against the planks and the geldings became startled when the wagon wheels loudly made contact with the hard surface of the narrow bridge. They charged ahead and the extra jolt sent the wagon over the edge of the bridge and Asa was thrown into the air. He landed at the bottom of the gully with the wagon on top of him. Asa could not move. Whenever he tried to change his position, the pain in his back was beyond tolerance. He calmed himself and waited for help to come. When his friends moved the wagon and started to lift Asa onto a cart, he passed out from the severe pain in his back. Thirteen days later, Asa Bishop passed away. On the death certificate, it read, "Cause of death: broken back." Emma Bishop was now a widow and little Ruth Bishop was without a father.

The months and years crept slowly by. Emma Bishop stood under the shade tree in her front yard and watched as the postman came down the street. The sun shot rays of light through the tree branches and cast golden streaks on her brown hair. Bellville, New York seemed at peace with the world. It was a safe, quiet college town composed mostly of old, retired farmers. The postman handed Emma a letter and she turned it over and over in her hands. It had arrived from Michigan and was postmarked with the year 1880. Emma strolled to the north porch where it would be cool. She sat in the huge, wicker rocker and started to open the letter. It was from her good friend, George Reader, who had gone in 1879 to see what Michigan was like.

Emma rested her head against the back of the rocker as she read Reader's letter. It had been a hard year and she was tired. Her teaching position at Belleville Public School and her little four-year-old daughter really kept her busy. She had to teach to support them both, and it was not easy to be both father and mother to a four year old little girl. Emma thought about the north wall of the parlor behind her. It was practically covered with pictures of her daughter. She knew that she would have to be careful that Ruth would not become a spoiled child. After all, there were quite a few people to help Ruth "get her own way." Her grandparents were always around, and then there was the lady that Emma had hired for five dollars a week to watch over Ruth while school was in session. Surrounded by grown-ups, Ruth had every chance in the world to be spoiled. She was known as her grandpa's "little pet."

Emma's eyes drank in the words of Reader's letter as he told about Michigan. The letter was full of excitement. Reader had made the trip from the state of New York and was looking for adventure and a nice place to settle. By late 1879, he had arrived in the little community of Sweetland in the northwest part of Michigan. [30] As soon as he arrived in the tiny community, Reader found employment in Hiram Scott's general store. The store was a very busy place because the train stopped there when necessary, and the mail was left there. Reader had the prestige of being assistant store manager, depot agent, postmaster, and whatever else was needed.

George Reader wrote all about the newly-settled community that he had come to and told Emma Bishop, or "Widow Bishop" as everyone had called her since her husband's untimely death, that a teacher was badly needed in the area. He informed Widow Bishop that this new territory would be ideal for her and he felt that she and her daughter would enjoy Sweetland, Michigan and Mason County as much as he did. Emma Bishop read and reread the letter many times, then placed it back in the envelope.

As Emma sat on the porch, she felt a slight breeze caress her left cheek. Turning her head in that direction, she closed her eyes and let her mind wander. Her thoughts traveled across the country to where George Reader was so happy and content. "Michigan," she mused half aloud, "Michigan." In her mind's eye, she visualized the topography of Michigan. It was as though God had gathered together everything that was good and molded it into a world; as though he had smoothed it here and there, making sure that none of his handprints were left upon it. Maybe, when he was satisfied with the results, God had tossed the world lightly toward the heavens where it hung gently amidst the white clouds and bright sunshine. Ruth smiled secretly to herself as she daydreamed about Michigan being God's last handprint on the world. Sweetland had grown and developed right at the base of the little finger on His print. As it was so close to the palm of God's hand, surely all of George Reader's praises for the area should not fall on unlistening ears. Emma leaned forward in the rocker and her own thoughts made a small smile dance at the corners of her lips and twinkle within her eyes. If the quiet, refined townfolk knew about some of her daydreams, they might wonder about their "schoolmar'm"! *That* thought made her chuckle aloud as she headed for the door.

After many months of deliberation, Emma decided to pack her family things, gather up her little daughter, and head for Michigan and a new life.

# —6—

# Sweetland, Michigan

LITTLE RUTH Bishop, picking up her long skirts, ran from one train window to another and gazed out. The train lurched with a choking gasp as if taking its last breath, and the wheels clanked to a stop. At last! She and her mother had arrived from New York State and would soon be setting foot on Michigan soil. Ruth wondered if they would be happy in Sweetland. As she pressed her nose flat against the train window and looked the area over, she felt that never in her young life had she seen such desolate country. The train smoke lifted skyward, but even then it revealed nothing but trees, trees, and more trees. The only cleared area was near the front of the train, near the window that she was peering through.

Two Indians with gunny sacks flung over their right shoulders passed by her train window. They had been to Scott's General Store for tobacco and a few supplies to take home to their squaws. Ruth watched as they started toward the river. She was fascinated by their walk. It seemed so different from the swagger of the white men. The Indians appeared to place the balls of their feet upon the ground first and then their heels. Their gait seemed so rythmic and silent. Ruth's mother had told her stories about how the Indians hunted the animals of the deep woods around Sweetland. No wonder the braves were such good hunters! They walked so silently. Ruth slid down from the window and practiced walking like an Indian. She silently moved up and down the train aisle. Her mother called to her and she followed obediently to the train door where they were greeted by the smiling face of George Reader. He had come to welcome them to Sweetland. Reader gathered Ruth up in his arms and conversed with her mother as he led the way to a room that had been prepared for them.

Ruth sat on the edge of the bed and gazed out the window. Here she was in Sweetland, Michigan. Her room was upstairs over Scott's General Store. Reader had taken her mother and her down to Sweetland's boardinghouse to see how soon there would be an empty room for them to move into. The boardinghouse was located on the southwest corner of what later became the crossroads of State and Main Streets. It was filled at that time with lumberjacks who were cutting the new road from Sweetland to Baldwin. When the road was completed, Sweetland literally became the crossroads of all Mason County, as the two main roads crossed right in the middle of the little village.

Ruth's eyes filled with tears as she looked north of the little community. At that time, Sweetland consisted of only one house, one boardinghouse, and five saloons north of the railroad tracks. The rest of the village lay south of the tracks and closer to the Père Marquette River. It was a pretty bleak outlook for a little four-year-old girl and as she lay back and buried her face in the pillow she thought, "Oh my, if I could only see Grandpa again!" After all, she had been able to see her grandparents every single day while her mother was teaching, and it seemed to be so very, very far back to the state of New York!

Ruth cried silently to herself and one lone tear slid noiselessly down her cheek. A loud guffaw made her sit bolt upright. She raced to the window and looked down on the main street. Three lumberjacks had left one saloon and went walking across the hard clay road to the second one. Apparently, one of them had said something quite humorous for the other two were laughing uproariously over whatever had been said. Ruth watched as all three tried to enter the saloon door at the same time. Reason seemed to seep into their fuzzed minds for they backed off and entered one at a time. As the second lumberjack held open the saloon door, the third man danced a jig through the opening accompanied by the player-piano music that was reverberating from the saloon. The whole affair struck Ruth as being very comical and she turned to tell Mama all about it. Her mother did not see the humor in the affair and told Ruth to go and play with her doll and that she did not want her watching uncouth folk like that ever again.

After a few days, Ruth and her mother were able to move into the local boardinghouse. They worked tediously to make their quarters more homelike. When they had finished, Emma Bishop and little Ruth stood in the center of the room and surveyed their handiwork. There were sheets most everywhere in the room. Ruth looked up at her mother's anxious face and began to fret silently. She was not sure that her mother really felt safe and secure here in the boardinghouse.

Their room was partitioned off in one corner of the first floor. It was the exact length and width of two bed sheets. Ruth's mother had taken two sheets and covered the complete ceiling of the room, because the boards were loose and dust, plus actual pieces of dirt, kept sifting down. The sifting was caused by the rough actions of the twelve lumbermen who resided above them. The sheets also helped to muffle the colorful language that the men used, and Emma Bishop certainly did not want Ruth to broaden her vocabulary with words such as those! Ruth ran to the bed and gathered up two more sheets for her mother to use. Emma Bishop stood on a chair and fastened the sheets across the entrance wall of the room. There was no door and the only way they had to lock their room was to pin the two sheets together with large safety pins. When the "walls" had been placed into position, Emma turned her attention toward the rest of the room. She placed two sheets and a large diamond-designed quilt over the feathertick on the high poster bed. Opening her own suitcase,

Ruth took her rag doll that Grandma had made for her and placed it on the quilt for a "rest." She took her other toys from the suitcase and searched in the bottom for her nightgown. Ruth knew that her mother would be wanting her to retire soon.

When the room was presentable, Ruth's mother helped her prepare for bed. As she tucked the quilt in around her little girl, Emma Bishop listened with furrowed brow to the loud laughter and booming voices that were reverberating throughout the whole building. She blew out the light, prepared for bed, and slid quietly in beside her small daughter. Emma put her arms around Ruth and felt her startled reaction as a lumberman's heavy shoe thudded noisily to the floor above them. Ruth started to whimper and Emma gathered her closer and spoke soft, comforting words to her. as she felt her young daughter's body relax in peaceful sleep, Emma said a silent prayer into the darkness of the room, "Please God, Thy will be done." As she stared into the blackness of the night, her thoughts returned again to the fact that the topography of Michigan was indeed like a large handprint; maybe even God's last handprint. Surely, she thought, if it were truly God's handprint on the earth, we are right on the edge of the palm itself and are absolutely safe! The idea pleased Emma. She smiled into the darkness, closed her eyes, and repeated her silent prayer. "Please God, Thy will be done." The room was quiet but for the screech of a passing nighthawk. The world truly seemed at peace.

# —7—

# "Schoolin' "

THE SUN rose high in the sky and the warmth could be felt as its rays caressed the furniture in the room. Emma Bishop sat stiffly in the parlor of the boardinghouse and faced the school board. She certainly did not agree with their plans and told them so very vehemently. They wanted her to teach only during the summer three-month session. Emma informed them that if she could not have a contract for the whole year, she would not take the position at all. The school board was fearful for her physical, as well as mental, welfare. They did not think that a mere woman could handle the larger boys who attended school. Quite a few of them were older Indian boys. Widow Bishop wanted the position as teacher so that she could support her daughter in the style that the good Lord would want her to. She informed the school board that she could manage the big boys without using her fist or a beech rod. She finally succeeded in getting the contract for one year. Emma received twenty-five dollars a month for wages and, besides teaching, she was expected to do her own janitor work. Widow Bishop was not unhappy about that. She was very content because she knew that having the teaching position would mean that her little daughter would be well cared for.

The local school was a log house located just one half mile north of town. Before that building came into being, only the older youth and the Indian boys attended school because it was too difficult for the younger set to travel to the former school. Before 1877, the nearest school to the little Père Marquette railway station was a small log building known as Jones School. It was located two miles as the crow flies northwest of town, and the children had to cross swamps and walk through forests to attend classes. The way was very rough and during bad weather  almost impossible. At that time, there were ten families in the district, because half of Sweetland was in Amber Township and the other half in Custer Township.

One afternoon, in the year 1877, a group of concerned men sat upon a woodpile near the southwest corner of where the main intersection of town would someday be found. Harry Melsom and H. Schulte had been the first to arrive and the two men watched as C. W. Jones, J. C. Mustard, James Sweetland, and John Winters arrived on the scene. Other men of the little village and nearby countryside joined the group. They talked over the weather and horse trading until J. N. Mack and Andrew Neil had arrived. It was not long before Winters cleared his throat, spit upon the hard clay road, and stated, "You men all know why we are here so let us get down to business." The group discussed the school situation and everyone felt that they needed a school closer to the area, so that the children would be better able to receive an education without so much physical hardship. After all, the younger children needed to learn "readin', writin', and 'rithmetic" also. Winters suggested that they do something about the situation, maybe even figure out a way to start a school right in the village. Each man nodded his head in approval, but no one knew just where the school should be placed, and certainly no one knew just where the money and material to build a school would come from.

The group of men just sat there and stared quietly at the activity going on within the village. No one knew what to say or do. John Winters stared, instead, at the furrowed brows and grim mouths of each man. He knew that they all were just as concerned as he, but an answer to the problem seemed to not

36

be in the offing. Winters said, "I'll do whatever I can to help in any way 'cause my young'uns need educatin' too." Herman Schulte looked at Winters and then swung his head around so that he could see the children who were laughing and playing under the maple trees near his home further down the street. Schulte turned back to Winters and said, "If you can furnish the lumber for a school, I will give my time as a carpenter but I will need some help." The men all looked at Schulte as he gave each one a questioning look concerning time to help. They were all so busy just plain supporting their families. That alone was a full time job from early morning until late at night. James Neil offered the use of an empty log house on his property just one half mile north of the village. Schulte informed the group that he would repair the building if they would all help as much as they could and would give as much time as they could spare. Every man at the meeting agreed to the idea. Thus, the first village school came into being.

The school year was divided into two sessions. The summer session consisted of three months, and Miss Bessie Bates was hired as teacher. Most of the small children were able to attend during the summer. C. W. Jones was engaged for the winter term of four months.[31] Sarah Turner followed Jones as teacher and taught during the summer of 1878.

No story of Scottville would be complete without the name of W. F. Fairbanks, who was one of the first teachers and also served in various village offices and as postmaster, at one time.[32] He was hired to fill the teaching position for the winter term of 1878-1879. Fairbanks used to wear slippers on his feet and he used the slippers for other purposes also. By 1878, the log schoolhouse had already become too small for the enrollment, which grew rapidly as more homesteaders came to the area. The southeast section of Cranley Corners, which was just a short distance from the log house that they had been using, looked like an ideal location for a new school. Cranley, a "horse and cow doctor", donated a corner of his land for the worthy cause. A new building was erected and

Fairbanks had the honor of becoming the first teacher to occupy the new school. He taught during the winter term while the big boys and Indians were in school. During 1879, Miss Flora Hill took charge of the school for the summer term. She was followed by a Mr. Stanton, who taught in the local school during the 1879-1880 winter term.

Thus it was that Emma Bishop, with all of her self confidence and fortitude, became the first woman teacher to be awarded a full year contract in the community's local school. Emma became quite influential in the community. She was a very active, community-minded individual and the next few years found her not only in the role of having been a schoolteacher but also a member of the county board of examiners, dressmaker, music teacher, nurse, assistant to the doctor whenever he came by, undertaker, and mother. In fact, she made herself so generally useful that even the village blacksmith stated that he could not get along without her. In August, 1882, he married her. Little Ruth Bishop not only gained a new father, she acquired a new brother as well. Elhanan Winchester Loomis had three married children away from home and a son who was six months older than Ruth. In fact, Irving Loomis and Ruth Bishop "stood up" with their parents when they were married.

The year 1882 found little Ruth Bishop ready to start her "formal schoolin'." As was stated earlier, the log schoolhouse at Cranley Corners had already proved to be too small for the growing enrollment and a new building was erected close by. It was in that new school that Ruth Bishop first started to gain her education.

Ruth's first day of school was one filled with excitement and yet a little apprehension. As her mother hooked the buttons on her high shoes and tied the wide sash on her dress, Ruth thought about going to school. She was very familiar with the school building itself. Her mother had taken Ruth with her when she taught because there was no one to care for the little girl. Ruth had to play quietly in the corner of the schoolroom and took her daily nap on a long wooden bench in the cozy area behind the pot-bellied stove that heated the building.

Ruth felt that it was wonderful to be old enough to attend school, but then her mother was no longer teaching and she had to be with strangers. As her mother helped her prepare for the big day, Ruth pondered over attending school without her mother. She stared at the floor while imaginary, wild thoughts raced through her mind and her eyes swam with held back tears. The rustle of her mother's long skirts brought her mind back to reality and she picked up her sunbonnet and shawl, took her mother's hand, and started out to face the unknown as only a six year old could visualize it.

Ruth's mother opened the schoolroom door and ushered her little, red haired daughter into the room. Ruth looked around apprehensively because she really did not know what to expect. She had heard wild tales about how the "big boys" acted at school. Mrs. C. D. Coddington had been awarded a year's contract as teacher following Emma Bishop. About two months before her school year was completed, she resigned and said, "It was because of the way the big boys acted." There was even talk about how the big boys would become angry at the younger ones, take them out behind the school, and try to stuff lit matches up their noses! Catherine Coburn took the reins and brought the school year to a blustery, but successful, finish. In 1882, Anna Coburn succeeded her sister as teacher and it was she who stepped forth to greet Emma Bishop and welcome Ruth Bishop in as a member of her student body.

Ruth looked around the classroom. Standing by the window was a young fellow with a big, friendly smile on his face. Ruth was happy to see him and felt more relaxed because she knew that she had, at least, one friend in the crowd. He was David Falconer, one of the boys who her mother had taught and who had told others that, "The teacher was all right, but she really had a nice little red-haired daughter!" (David Falconer later became Ruth Bishop's husband.) Ruth sat down on one of the benches. There were rows of long, handmade, high-backed benches in the room with desks in front of them. Up front was a large platform which held the teacher's desk and the globe. Miss Coburn usually stayed up on the platform when teaching. The toilets were out behind the school and were marked "boys" and "girls." The big honor of the day was to be water boy or girl. When youngsters would get thirsty or just plain want an excuse to skip classes, they would ask to be in charge of water. The honored one was allowed to carry the water pail up and down the rows of students. Each one took the long handled dipper, drank from it, and passed it on to the next student. When empty, the dipper was refilled from the pail which, in turn, was refilled at the well out behind the schoolhouse.

The school year of 1883-1884 found H. E. Scott behind the teacher's desk. In the year 1884, after being out of the teaching field for five years, W. F. Fairbanks served as teacher. He was considered to be one of the best mathematicians of his time. In 1885, A. P. Starke, who was noted for thrashing even his own children at school, wielded the beech rod for one year.[33]

During that time, the town folk realized that the school had, again, become too small for the growing enrollment of children. In 1886, the school board rented a room in the house of Nellie Watrus and hired her to teach the little, or chart class, children. Charles Hill, a member of the school board, installed his daughter in a house on East State Street and the school board hired her to teach the fourth and fifth grades of the local school system. Hill took his school board position quite seriously and each morning he would show up at school to give the day's directions to his daughter. One day he would come with beech rods and tell his daughter to thrash the children if they needed it. The next day he would show up and direct her not to touch them, no matter what they did. All this was very frightening to the children for, as the new day dawned, they never knew what to expect. The sixth grade and older still attended the Cranley Corners school. Lawyer E. J. Richmond taught the last year that the dwelling was used as a schoolhouse at that location. He was considered a very good teacher, but no one ever saw him smile.[34] The Cranley Corners School building was later sold, moved to the southern part of the village, and used as a hall where the local Lithuanians met.

"Strike three! You're out!" called the umpire. David Falconer tossed the bat down harder than he intended and it bounded over by the tall grass at the edge of the field. He looked up and saw twelve-year-old, red-haired Ruth Bishop and her friends watching him walk away from the batter's box. He wished that he had been able to at least hit the ball. After all, it was the first ball game that they had ever played on the playground of the new brick school. (The year was 1888 and the school at Cranley Corners had proved to be too small for the growing enrollment. A new brick building was built on the northwest side of Main Street, and the old school was sold.)

David walked over to ask Ruth Bishop about her new adopted sister. He had tried to think of a good excuse to stop and talk to her. Her new sister surely seemed like a plausible enough reason. The baby girl's mother had passed away and Ruth's mother had taken the youngest of the five children that had been left behind. After a period of time, Ruth's family adopted the little girl as their own. She was almost twelve years younger than Ruth. Her name was Olive Patterson, but the family renamed her Via A. Loomis to show that she had been obtained "via adoption"!

After discussing Via, the topic of conversation shifted to their new school. David and the girls turned to gaze at the new building. It was a two-story structure and each floor consisted of a large room sandwiched between two small hallways which ran down each side. The hallways consisted of the stairs, plus a long cloakroom which housed the students' wraps and lunch pails. The large classrooms held the desks for the teachers and students. In one corner was the water pail and dipper which had to be filled three times a day from the pump. As in the old school building, the children all used the same dipper to obtain water from the pails to quench their thirst. A student

41

would take a drink from the dipper and pass it on for the next student to sip from. Thus no water was wasted and not as much pumping was necessary. Much to everyone's delight, in 1897, the village acquired piped, running water and the children only had to turn a faucet to obtain all the cool, fresh water they could have ever wished for.

Overhead in the classrooms were two "drop-type" hanging kerosene lamps with huge, oval-shaped reflectors over them to cast the light downward for the students' benefit. The building was flanked by two small outhouses, one marked "His" and one "Hers." Right behind the schoolhouse was the pump where the water was obtained to fill the drinking water pails. Russ Parker had the honor of being the first teacher hired for the new brick school. The first eighth grade graduation was held in 1893, with eight students graduating. Ruth Bishop was one of the graduates. In 1903, the school held its first twelfth grade graduation, with two students graduating. Nora Cranley and Pearl Shelly were the two who received their twelfth grade diplomas that year.[35]

The brick schoolhouse proved to be too small to accommodate the large number of pupils at that time, but the school board put up with the conditions for a couple of years. Then a little wooden building was built just north of the central building. The first three grades were placed in the small building. Even with the additional space, there was still an overflow of pupils and the next move was the renting of the G.A.R. or Odd Fellows building which housed some of the children until 1903 when an addition was built on the front of the brick school. During the year 1911, north and south wings were added to the building.[36]

In 1927, a gymnasium was added to the school. Basketball, whose history began in 1891, had already made its debut in town. E. M. Briggs arrived as a young man in 1886, from Syracuse, New York, and it was not long before the Briggs Hardware store came into being. Before its development, though, Briggs built two large buildings bordering on the north side of the railroad tracks between Reinberg Avenue and Main Street. The east building was used to house the Briggs Lumber Company while the larger west building boasted a hardwood floor, and it was in that building, a few years later, that the local athletes held their basketball games. The building was feebly heated by a pot-bellied stove which had been placed in one corner. There were no bleachers to sit on so the town folk just crowded in and leaned against the waist-high railing that ran parallel to the walls of the huge room. From that vantage point, they cheered lustily and shouted encouragement to their favorite team. Even before the days of basketball, though, the Briggs building had really been dubbed the entertainment center of the village. It was considered to be a roller skating rink, and skates could be rented by a young swain to squire his favorite girl to a "whirl on wheels." At one time, the attraction was a skating bear. The local folks would lean against the waist-high railing with mouths agape in disbelief as the trainer put his skating bear through the act of gliding over the floor on roller skates. Another entertainment that titillated the pleasure seekers of that day were the man versus bear wrestling matches that were held in the Briggs building. Protective strips were placed over the bear's claws and the call went out for any young man who felt that he was robust and rugged enough to wrestle the "man wrestling" bear. Many were the stories told to grandchildren, in later years, concerning these "bear events."

With the building of a new gymnasium, most of the social affairs that concerned teenagers were then held at the school. There were different church groups and social clubs that the city folk belonged to, but the "going thing" in 1916 was the newly formed Parent-Teachers Association which blossomed forth under the guidance of Mrs. Lewis Hunt, mother of Dr. Ivan Hunt who became one of the local doctors in later years, and who officiated when the author first saw the light of day. It did not take the Parent-Teacher Association very long to move their monthly meetings into the new gymnasium, their pride and joy.

By 1955, the school system employed twenty-three

teachers, two secretaries, and two maintenance men. There were also seven districts annexed to the school district and it was growing very rapidly.[38] The annexation did not literally fall into place quietly. Every district that had the urge to annex to Scottville, went through a time of numerous meetings and discussions. At times, the differences in opinion became very evident. The author herself can remember one such meeting at a rural school northeast of town, when her own father stood up and said, "I move that we annex to the Scottville School District." Another gentleman in the crowd jumped up and shouted in anger, "What are you—a Nazi?" The district did annex and all went well, but such incidents were long remembered with much mirth.

By 1956, the school system had changed its name to Mason County Central Schools and had more than one thousand students enrolled in classes.[39] In 1959, a new high school blossomed forth on the northwest side of town. It was located on an eighteen-acre tract of land. A lot of credit for the fine structure must be given to Arnold O. Carlson, who taught in the local school for thirty-nine years, of which thirty-two were as superintendent of the school system.[40] In fact, in 1942, he handed the author a high school diploma on graduation day.

Carlson was considered a friend by each and every student, and yet he demanded their respect. The youngsters could feel the warmth of his friendship when they conversed with him, but even so there was something about him that held them in awe. Every student under Carlson's superintendency would long remember the school assemblies when some courageous or cowardly, whichever preferred, student had gone astray. The following is one such incident.

The students pushed and shoved noisely into the gymnasium. They chattered happily as they greeted friends from other classes. Arnold O. Carlson walked into the gymnasium and faced the assembly. The students, without outside prompting, became respectfully still. After pacing back and forth for a few moments as if in deep meditation, Carlson

44

picked up a chair and took it to the center of the floor so that he could sit down to talk. He had a tall, lean frame and had the habit of wrapping his long arms about his body and entwining his legs around the chair not unlike a pretzel. Having completed that, he began to talk, saying, "No man in this world loves his wife any more than I. Loving her as I do, I also have deep respect for her. Never, ever, would I walk down the halls of this school, or anywhere else, and paw her in public. I do not feel that any young man in this room has the right to degrade any young lady of our school system by pawing and necking her in public. I am not asking that you refrain from doing this. I am telling you to stop it and I mean as of this moment on. Such actions will not be tolerated in our Mason County Central Schools. We will all have respect for each other as human beings, not as playthings. Are there any questions?" A quiet, but respectful group of students returned to their classes. In years to come, Arnold O. Carlson would long be remembered by many as one of the fine pillars of our local school system.

Due to annexation to the Scottville school system of outlying country schools, the enrollment kept mushrooming and since the mid 1950s, the district has built two new elementary buildings in addition to the new high school and converted the old two-story brick building into a "middle school" for only the sixth, seventh, and eighth grades. Later, four portable classrooms were moved in to house the sixth grade. Before too many years have passed, the author assumes that more progress will have been made and more building completed. In fact, at the time of completion of this book, plans had already been formulated for a new "middle school" to be built immediately north of the high school. History will always be full of the building of new schools and the educating of children. As Bismarck once wrote; "The nation that has the schools has the future."

# Sadness, Sickness, and Sorrow

BY 1882, the little village had become a most enterprising and busy place. Known first as Sweetland, so named for one of the mill owners in the community, it was also called Mason Center by some folks because of its location. The local residents, of the tiny village all called it Sweetland.[41] By late 1882, the whole area had been shocked by a great local scandal and the name of the village was immediately changed from Sweetland to Scottville.

Ruth Bishop was just a small child when "the scandal" happened. She and her mother still lived in Sweetland's boardinghouse, and so were in the same building that housed the scandal. Mr. and Mrs. Sweetland ran the boardinghouse for the government. Ruth watched her mother's body bristle with indignation as she paced back and forth in their room. Her mother muttered to herself about it being the most terrible thing that could have happened; she certainly did not approve of it; and she could not understand whatever possessed a man to do such a horrible thing. She told Ruth to stay in their room and play while she went in and, as she put it, "Someone should sympathize with Mrs. Sweetland, the poor soul." James Sweetland's wife had given birth to twin daughters and, while she was still bedridden, Sweetland ran off with an Indian squaw and never returned. He died, years later, in the state of New York.

47

Everyone felt very indignant over Sweetland's actions and the disgrace that he had brought to his family and to the village. The next day, Ruth watched her mother as she prepared to go to the village meeting. She wanted to go along and so her mother allowed her to do so. At the meeting, all of the townfolk agreed that something had to be done to "right the wrong." George Reader and Hiram Scott stated that they would not live in a place named for a man who would do such a deed as that. So Hiram Scott and his business manager, George Reader, tossed a coin on the main corners of town (where the stoplight would one day be located). Scott won the honor of renaming the village and so he named Scottville. Reader named State and Main Streets.[42] A few years later, Reader was also instrumental in getting the village incorporated.[43]

Thus, Scottville was named for Hiram Scott, an outstanding man in many ways and, according to Mrs. Scott, the finest man that ever lived. He taught school and shipped lumber, tan bark, potatoes, maple sugar, and anything else available. Being a very considerate man and easy going, Scott strongly trusted everyone and gave too much credit, which caused him to close his retail business in bankruptcy.[44] In late 1882, Charles Blaine and Hiram Scott platted the area. The first real streets to be constructed were Blaine, Crowley, State, and Main. Some town folk considered it very interesting to observe how the village fathers named everything after themselves or their closest friends.

The years 1881 and 1882 would long be remembered as the time that the diptheria epidemic struck Mason County. Everyone was very frightened by the whole affair and would do almost anything to avoid contact with the disease. By the spring of 1882, it had found its way to the little village in the most central part of the county. The Andrew Neil family, with seven children, lived near Cranley Corners on the northwest side of town. One night, two of their children came down with diptheria. Neil and his wife were very frightened. As the

48

family sat huddled in the lamp-lit kitchen, they discussed what would be best for everyone concerned. Mrs. Neil said that she would stay in the house and care for her sick children while Neil took the rest of them out to stay in the corncrib. Maybe that way the rest would avoid getting the illness. Neil herded the children into the corncrib and that is where they stayed until the diptheria nightmare had passed from their home. The Neil family lost three of their children during the epidemic.

A few nights later, Ruth Bishop was awakened by a loud knock on their door. Since her mother had married "Father Loomis," the family had lived upstairs over his blacksmith shop which was located on the east side of Main Street in the very center of town. Ruth had spent the whole day downstairs watching her new-found father work the bellows, wield the anvil, and shape the shoes for the horses. She did not move when a second, more persistent knock sounded because she was quite tired and knew that her parents would answer the door. The sound of a man's fear-filled, sobbing voice made her bolt from her bed. It was a resident of "Po-Dunk Row" which was a small lane, or alley, through the edge of town lined with a row of shabby houses covered overall by a single long roof. The poorer people lived there. Ruth heard her mother hurry to the door. She tiptoed to the window so that she could hear what was being said. The man needed help. One man in Po-Dunk Row had just died from diptheria and two more were, as he put it, "a-standin' at the door o' death!" Loomis and his wife hurriedly dressed and rushed over to help. Little Ruth crept back to bed, pulled the warm blankets up to her chin, and thought about their box at the new post office just southeast of Scott's General Store. She surely hoped that she would soon receive another letter from Grandpa, back there in safe New York State.

Before the sun rose to welcome a new day, all three men in Po-Dunk Row had died and left families to mourn them. Loomis and some of the other local men built three green hemlock coffins that day in which to bury the victims and

Emma Loomis, formerly Emma Bishop, took black alpaca dress material that she had purchased years before in New York and pleated it around the outside of the coffins, so that the poor souls would have a more decent burial.

Ruth Bishop would never forget the fear and tension that gripped everyone when someone whispered the word, "diptheria." School was closed for weeks and social gatherings were nil. Due to bad roads and poor weather, there was only one doctor available in the area who would consider coming to the village, and he was eight miles away! The other doctors did not appreciate traveling so far and over such rugged roads; then too, they had diptheria epidemics in their own villages. Even the county seat down by Lake Michigan was suffering from an epidemic!

Ruth's mother was a very busy person. She seemed to be the only one who had no great fear of the disease. Emma traveled from home to home, helping wherever she was needed. She had a few bottles of "puncturing fluid" which she had acquired while working with the German doctor back in the state of New York. When folks showed the very first signs of coming down with diptheria, Emma would rub their necks and chests with "puncturing fluid," then hold a coal shovel full of hot coals as close under their chins as possible. She would keep it there until the hot coals made the fluid bubble and "yellow festers" would break out. This, she felt, was drawing the diptheria right out of them. Emma Loomis, the former Widow Bishop, was credited with saving quite a few lives during the epidemic. Her young daughter looked upon her as a real heroine.

The year was 1883, and Scottville appeared to be at peace with itself and the world in general. The early evening was very still, except for a lone nighthawk here and there that would swoop down by the rooftops and vent forth its shrill cry. Ruth and her family sat and listened to the sounds of the birds, then talked over plans for the next day. It was not long before they had retired and were sleeping soundly. No one was aware that

**50**

still more sadness lurked within the dark shadows of the night. Ruth's stepfather, Elhanan Loomis, was not aware that they were in danger in any way. Suddenly, the whole family was jolted out of sound sleep by the frantic cry of "Fire! Fire!" The blacksmith shop was on fire. The fire had started in some sawdust behind the building and had slowly eaten its way into the building itself. Ruth sat up in bed with utter disbelief written upon her face. She threw back the quilt and flannel sheet that covered her and jumped from her bed. With panic pounding within her heart, she raced to the window. Ruth could see flames licking up the side of the building. Her stepbrother Irving was so upset and shocked that he dressed himself in his very best clothes and grabbed his bag of marbles to take with him. He was later found on his knees down on the dirt street, playing marbles. He seemed in a daze and not at all aware of what he was doing.

Ruth raced out in her nightgown. Her mother handed her a glass globe filled with wax fruit that she had made back before Civil War days in the state of New York. Emma told her daughter, "Ruth, take this fruit arrangement and put it in a corner of the fence by Mrs. Schulte's lot." She took the fruit and did what her mother had told her to do. (In 1973, the fruit arrangement was given to the Mason County Historical Society and was placed in the county museum to be viewed by all.) Loomis and his family saved most of their small valuables, but everything else was destroyed by fire. Ruth's mother was very thankful that most of her furniture was still back in the state of New York and had escaped the fire. She later had her furniture shipped to her.

Ruth leaned back in the porch swing and listened to "Uncle George" and "Aunt Kate" as they talked to her mother about the terrible fire. They were sitting on the wide porch of the Andre Hotel and could see the black rubble that was still smoldering down the street. That black rubble had been her home. Ruth pulled her eyes from the horrible, frightening scene and looked around her. She listened as her mother said,

51

"Aunt Kate, thank goodness for the Andre Hotel!" The hotel was less than a year old and had been built on the northeast corner of State and Main Streets.[45] It was managed by George and Kate Andre, who were affectionately called "Uncle George and Aunt Kate" by all of the children in town. The adults called her "Aunt Kate" as the children did, but they called him "Big George." He was a huge man of German descent and had a booming voice to match his size. In fact, he was such a large man that when he left this earthly world they had to remove the door casings to get his casket out of the hotel.

Ruth walked down off of the porch and strolled across the yard to a big maple tree that stood nearby. She turned around and looked back at the porches that extended on both the Main and State Street sides of the building. Besides being used by travelers who might stay at the hotel, the huge porches were used by local residents as well. It was a comfortable, pleasant and friendly place to meet and discuss the happenings of the day.[46] "Uncle George" allowed the Loomis family to have two rooms downstairs and one room upstairs. They lived there until they had built their new home on East State Street. Their home was built right next to where the Schulte home would one day be moved. In later years, it seemed quite fitting that these two pioneer homes had been placed side by side. If they could talk, they would have many interesting reminiscences to relate.[47] The Loomis family moved into their new home a little over one year after fire devoured the blacksmith shop.

So it was that the sadness of a town scandal, a sickness called diptheria, and the sorrow of a home lost to the hungry licks of a raging fire were all to be long remembered in the mind and heart of Ruth Bishop, the little red-haired girl from New York State.

—9—

# Indian Tales

THE AUTHOR has not written very much about the Indians that were in the area during the late 1870s and early 1880s. About that same time in history, the Indians of the West were having trouble in the Black Hills of North Dakota. Gold seekers were pouring in and the Sioux Indians, led by Chiefs Sitting Bull and Crazy Horse, were not about to let them stay. The year 1876 saw the blood of Custer's Last Stand color the green grass a brilliant red. Custer had foolishly led 264 soldiers to their deaths.[48] The Custer episode did not have much effect on the folk of the area; in fact, they were not aware of all that had happened and the "wild, wild West" seemed so far away. It might be thought that, by then, the local Indians were extinct. This was not true. Some of them had moved or scattered to parts unknown, but others were definitely still there. An Indian brave could be seen paddling his canoe up the Père Marquette River or coming to the village for supplies.

One bright day in 1889, an Indian brave entered the Reader's Hardware Store which was located in the center of the block on the west side of Main Street. He strolled up to a local farmer and started to talk about a horse that he wanted to trade. The Indians were always making horse deals with the men of the village and the nearby farmers. After much discussion, the two men got into a quarrel over a horse trade and they could not come to an agreement. Finally, tempers flew and the farmer picked up a plow handle and hit the Indian over the head with it. Everyone thought that he had killed the red man right there in the store, so some of the local men who had witnessed the incident picked the Indian up and carried him across the street to Elhanan Loomis' shop. There was a fourteen-year-old boy who had seen the whole thing and he followed the crowd to Loomis' new blacksmith shop.

Ruth Bishop was thirteen years old at the time, and she saw the crowd of men carrying the bloody Indian toward her stepfather's place of business. She raced inside and told Loomis that they were coming. Ruth noticed her stepfather's rifle as it leaned against the wall. It had a barrel "as large as a cowhorn" and looked mighty huge to Ruth. She picked it up and handed it to Loomis. She did not know if he would need it or not. The men laid the Indian on some wood shavings in the shop and propped his head up with a wooden block. The Indian moaned and began moving his hands so everyone knew that he was still alive. Ruth and the boy stood in the door and watched the proceedings. Suddenly the Indian's body gave a violent jerk. He let out a little sigh and died. Slowly and quietly, the men moved toward the door and left the building. When they had a trial concerning the affair, the boy was called as a state's witness. Ruth was considered to be too young so she did not have to testify. The farmer was convicted and spent quite a few years in prison for the murder of the Indian. The farmer's relatives lived quite near town, and in later years he came back to see them but did not dare to show his face in town as the other Indians had threatened to scalp him on the spot.

As time passed the community changed, and it was not long before there were not too many in town who remembered the incident. The farmer was released from prison and came back to spend his last years in Scottville. His daughter was quite prominent in the community by that time, because she had married a local druggist. She gave a golden wedding anniversary party for her parents. It was a gala, social affair and everyone in town was invited — except Fred Reader and Emma Loomis. They were not invited because of their relationship to the tragic incident. While the whole town was at the party, Reader went over to talk to Emma Loomis. He mentioned that he was not angry because they did not invite him to the party. He said, "After all, I would not have known what to buy that farmer except a gold-plated plow handle!"

Another incident concerning the local Indians happened one Fourth of July and involved the red man's use of the white man's "firewater." The pioneers had gathered in the village and were having a wonderful time celebrating the holiday. A wooden platform had been constructed in the center of town and the fiddler sat in one corner filling the air with lively music while the dancing couples swayed this way and that. Much to everyone's amusement, the fiddler was keeping time by tapping his foot and allowing his bushy eyebrows to dance up and down on his forehead while his mustache quivered rhythmically on his upper lip. Everyone, including the Indians, was filled with happiness and a feeling of fun concerning the occasion.

It was not long before the young braves had consumed more than their share of the "firewater." Some of them became quite inebriated and soon were in a state of unconsciousness. Their kinfolk laid them in a row along the edge of the boardwalks so that they could "sleep it off." Some of the pioneer youth of the day decided to see some fireworks of their own making. They set the sleeping Indians' hair afire! The braves were too far under the influence of alcohol to realize what had happened and others nearby had to put the flames out for them. Ruth and some of her friends watched as the young pioneer youths raced off laughing. The girls were very shocked over the whole incident and they all ran for home. Ruth raced into the house and breathlessly told her mother what had happened. She was so afraid that there was going to be a war with the Indians. Everything went on as usual though and the incident did not carry any aftermath.

On another evening in that same period, some of the braves from a local Indian camp came into the village for a little relaxation. Again, they consumed too much of the white man's alcoholic beverage. On their way back to their homes, they became quite happy and thought that they would have a little fun. The braves came upon a pioneer home, not knowing that the mother of the family was home alone with her tiny baby. With a whoop and a holler, they circled the home and did a fancy Indian dance around it as they screamed, yelled, and shot arrows through the windows. The young pioneer mother was certainly terrified! When morning came, the chief of the tribe visited the pioneer home, apologized for his braves' actions, and promised the family that this sort of thing would never happen again.

Although there were quite a few such incidents throughout the early history of Scottville, the red man did not seem to resent the invasion of the white pioneers. In fact, they adopted more and more of the white man's living habits. In later years, the Indian village between Custer and Scottville was found to be deserted. The red man had blended in completely with his white brother. They were considered to be friends, neighbors, and truly Americans.

# —10—

## Time for Prayer

DURING THE night, mother nature had completed her laundry and the brilliant Sunday morning sun found the world refreshed and clean. Drops of rain on the leaves and petals glistened here and there in the warm sun like tiny diamonds. Ruth noticed how beautiful everything looked as she and her mother walked to school that morning. They were on their way to attend church.

Ruth cast her eyes toward the edge of the dirt road and looked for a big turtle. She and some of her friends had come across huge mud turtles on their way to the schoolhouse on different mornings and had taken turns standing on the turtles' large, hard shells for a slow "ride" to school. As her eyes searched the weeds by the roadside, Ruth wondered how her mother would react to seeing a turtle. Sometimes mothers were not too impressed with turtles, snakes, and other such friends. Ruth's mother gave her hand a tug and warned Ruth that they would be late for church if she did not quit dilly-dallying around.

In the year 1882 there was no church in town, and services were held in the schoolhouse. Most of the folk scattered around the little village were Free Methodists and held very zealous and lively church services. Ruth and her mother were Baptists, but there was no Baptist church "short o'

Ludington," so they attended services in the school with everyone else.

Ruth went in and sat down while her eyes searched out Reverend Waumsley. Even though it frightened her a little, she wanted to watch him. He really "had the power," and shouted loudly as he raced about. Time after time, he would jump up on the platform, clap his hands together three times and shout, "Praise the Lord! Praise the Lord! Praise the Lord!" before he would ever hit the floor again. Ruth would try to mimic him and tell other boys and girls who did not attend church how he did it, but they would not believe her. She would tell them, "I have seen him do it many, many times so that is no squibbin' at all."

It was not long before the folks decided that they needed a regular church building. In 1883, they built the Peoples' Church just one half block east of the main corners of town. It was called Peoples' Church because all denominations worshipped there. They had one minister and then another from different denominations and that lasted for quite awhile until they sold it to the Church of the Brethren who held services there until their new church was built south of Custer.

There was no formal, legal organization of the Methodist Church in town until the year 1884. Services were held in Welch's Opera House which was located on the second floor above Welch's Bakery on the east side of Main Street. Ruth and her mother attended services there, and Ruth's mother purchased a marble-topped communion table from Shackleton's Furniture in Ludington and presented it to the church. The Sunday School had a large attendance, and the church seemed to be the center of a good deal of the village's social life as well as being characterized by a deep evangelistic spirit. In later years, flames licked their way through Welch's Opera House and in 1890, the First Methodist Church was built on West State Street.[49]

Ruth would long remember the Methodist Church and how proud everyone was of it. There were long, wooden pews

58

and a fine piano up front. A pot-bellied stove furnished warmth for the services and everyone would huddle around it until the minister made the announcement that church was ready to begin. The pianist would hit a chord on the piano and that was the notice for all small children to "git" with their parents and settle down for a time of holy worship. All would sit with bowed heads as the church bell pealed forth its glad message that Sunday morning had again arrived. Then the congregation could be heard even through the closed windows as they sang some of the old gospel hymns.

Although they were Baptists, Ruth and her mother attended the Methodist Church each and every Communion Sunday, as well as on all other days of worship. Because the church had open communion, Ruth pledged her life to God whenever communion was offered. Two ushers would go forth to the communion table and bring the bread and grape juice to the people in the pews. The plates of broken bread were passed up and down the rows of worshippers; then it was time for the grape beverage. The ushers each held a large, ornate glass and a beautiful pitcher full of the juice. The usher would fill his large glass and it was passed down the full length of the pew with each and every person sipping from it and passing it on to the next. This continued until the glass was completely empty and then it was returned to the usher to be refilled.

In 1890, the Methodist Parsonage was only a one-story building. By 1901, it had been raised and changed into a two-story structure. In the fall of 1911, the basement was built and a furnace installed. The present Methodist Church was erected in 1924 at a cost of a little over twenty-four thousand dollars. It was built on the same location as the original Methodist Church.

The author has written more about the Methodist Church than any other because it was the one Ruth was most involved with. There were many other churches that made their debut in the village as years went by. The year 1888 saw the erection of the Evangelical Church in the area. The Catholic Church was constructed in 1910 on West State Street right next to

McPhail field.[50] Mrs. B. A. Schulte was instrumental in helping to organize the Catholic Church in the village. Generations of the Schulte family would long be faithful members of the Catholic Church. They were all descendants of Bertram A. Schulte, the first white child to be born in the village, and of Herman Schulte, an experienced carpenter who built many of the first churches and homes in the Scottville area. By 1974, Sunday morning services were being held in five churches within the city limits of Scottville. There were various active churches in the surrounding countryside as well.

In early days, just as today, not all religious ceremonies were practiced in churches. A lot of funerals were held in homes. Wakes for the deceased were a common practice, and someone sat up all night with the departed one before the burial day. So it was in 1889 when Ruth's stepbrother, Irving Loomis, passed away from typhoid fever. The evening before Irving's funeral was cloudy, making the sky appear darker than usual. The wind began to blow with increasing force and hissed through the trees; it sounded like a shriek. Big drops of rain started to fall and as the drops became more numerous, the wind died down. The storm had moved inland from Lake Michigan.

Ruth's whole family was shocked by Irving's death. They certainly did not expect to have the thirteen-year-old boy leave their midst at such a young age. Ruth sat on a chair in the parlor and watched her parents. Everything seemed a little spooky. They were talking in such low tones; almost whispering.

Ruth did not like funerals and certainly did not look forward to another one. There had been the funeral for Mrs. Mead's little one-year-old daughter, Margaret. The Mead girl would never know that she was the first person to be buried in what someday would be Scottville's Brookside Cemetery. Before then, people were buried near their own homes, by a favorite stream, in the orchard, or near the woods. After the cemetery was started, folks moved their relatives to it for re-burial so some headstones do date before Margaret's. In

**60**

checking, though, the author found that the earlier dates were definitely on graves of folks who were moved to the cemetery years after they had died and been buried elsewhere.

Ruth watched Father Loomis light the lamps that hung on the wall and he turned the pie-pan-shaped reflectors just a little so that the light would be cast more toward Irving's coffin. Ruth turned toward the coffin and her gaze traveled from the foot of it up to Irving's somber face which showed white above the black cloth that covered the lower part of his body. She mused to herself, "Oh, this whole affair is really quite frightening! I must remember, though, that Mama said Irving is now in heaven and not there in that bleak box. He is probably playing marbles in heaven just as he loved to do here!" That thought made Ruth feel more comfortable about even the funeral itself.

Loomis went outside and brought in some long planks. Ruth's mother placed some chairs in different locations in the parlor and they laid the long planks on the chairs. There had to be plenty of room for friends to come for Irving's funeral the next day. Ruth walked into the kitchen and saw all of the pies, cakes, and cookies that the neighbors had brought in to help her mother during such a trying time. She sampled a huge sugar cookie and, picking up the lamp, she headed back toward the parlor so that she would be able to tell her parents that she was going to bed. The next day, Irving was buried next to his real mother in a cemetary down by Pentwater.

Not long after that, Ruth's mother was asked to furnish the music for another funeral just west of town at what was later known as the Felt Farm. She did not want to go alone, so a reluctant Ruth went with her. As her mother played the organ, Ruth sat on a chair in one corner and watched the whole episode. Again, long planks had been placed on chairs for the mourners. While the organ gave forth soft music, friends and neighbors of the deceased came slowly in and sat on the planks. Ruth noticed that the room was really very small. Her mother's back actually touched the edge of the coffin as she sat playing the organ! She did not appreciate that!

61

All went quite smoothly and everything seemed quiet and low keyed. Suddenly, as the service ended, the minister said in a loud voice, "Well, if everybody's seen the remnants, down goes the kiver!" He slammed the coffin shut. Ruth was so shocked by what had taken place, she cried all the way home and was to remember the whole affair for the rest of her life.

It is true that the religious events and churches of days gone by have left their mark in a positive, moral way on the little village that became Scottville, Michigan. If folks of the past could converse with the Scottville residents of the future, they would probably hope that religions to come might mean as much to future generations as theirs did to them. They would more than likely say about the religion of their day, "It was so; and it was good."

# —11—

# Growth and Change

WHILE ALL the steady progress was going on in Scottville, the post office department was not standing still. The local office moved out of the Scott store in 1880 and settled in a building across the street just to the southeast. Chauncey Richert was the first real postmaster.[51] Later, C. W. Jones became postmaster and the office was moved west across the street to the store where the Scottville cream station had been. Since that time, the post office has been moved to five different locations in town and, finally, settled permanently in a new building constructed in 1959 on the same location where it had been when C. W. Jones was postmaster.

Besides having a permanent place for the town folk to receive their mail, the first rural delivery was started out of Scottville in 1901. This grew rapidly until there were four routes being served. Many folks can remember the horse-drawn, square-box delivery wagons, with wheels in the summer and bob sleighs in the winter. A tiny stove had been placed for heat in each wagon with smoke pipes extending out of the back. The smoke literally rolled out whenever the mailman refueled. It was quite a sight to see as it jogged along over mud-rutted roads in the spring and snow-piled roads in the winter. William Quinn was one of the first rural mail carriers. Upon the arrival of cars and the improvement of roads, the four routes were soon combined into two.[52] In 1974, route one traversed the land south of the Père Marquette River while route two ran north of the river.

There were many humorous stories told of the hardships that the early mail carriers went through. The late Mrs. William Robinson frequently recalled how she had walked much of route four when she accompanied Robinson on his route to help him in the deep sand and mud. Many of the rural folk also told of the kindness of the rural carriers when there were few cars, few telephones, and hard traveling. At times, the carrier would bring medicine, food, or even kerosene for lamps.[53] To many a lonely farm family the big highlight of the day was when the mailman came. This kept them in touch with the world in general and made the long, cold winters seem to go by much faster.

Until about 1936, all mail came in by train, but later it entered the city by truck and the trains did not carry mail at all anymore. On November 4, 1949, the new highway post office service started operating on the Saginaw-Ludington and Grand Rapids-Manistee routes. It was very convenient that both of the routes passed right through Scottville. The modern "mail cars of the highway" marked but another step in the transition from horse and buggy days. City delivery in Scottville was established in 1918. The first city carrier was William Griffin.[54]

Outstanding for their long years of service in the Scottville Post Office were J. J. Cox, Miss Hattie Baltzer, and J. Ralph Reeds. Not only did they give years of service to the postal department, they were also all very active in community affairs and community progress.

In 1884, the *Mason Center Advocate* was the newspaper being read by the citizens of the village. It had the honor of being the first paper to be published in Scottville and John Bryan was its editor.

All newspapers in 1885 told of the bad winter and the great loss of cattle out west, which was really the beginning of the end for the great "Cattle Boom."[55] The news was also found in the *Mason County Enterprise* which was then the local newspaper. In 1889, Scottville had three newspapers besides the *Enterprise*. They were the *County Republican,* the *County Democrat,* and a prohibition paper. The *Enterprise* was edited continuously until it merged with the *Ludington Daily News.* The other three papers mentioned were very short-lived and after the *Enterprise* had combined with the *Ludington Daily News,* Scottville was without a paper for some time.[56]

The next five years saw papers with different titles started and ended until Harry Kruse of Manistee came to town. On August 24, 1938, Kruse put out his first edition of the *Mason County Press.*[57] He published the paper for nine years until Orin Kaye took over the helm. Kaye's son followed him as editor, with Clayton Spencer following in his footsteps. The two local papers to be found on town porches in years to come were the *Ludington Daily News* and the *Mason County Press,* which made weekly appearances.

Some of the articles that were printed in the early newspapers were quite humorous. For instance, one headline stated, "Hotel Burns; One Thousand Lives Lost." The hotel had the reputation of having bedbugs and it was the bedbugs which had perished! The village was not too large and the editor had to find all the news that he could possibly glean from anywhere. Another such article was found in the Thursday, March 15, 1917 issue of the *Scottville Enterprise.* It read as follows:

> Ellsworth Newcombe, 38, who says he is a barber from Custer, came to Manistee last Friday to "have a good time," says the *Manistee News-Advocate* of Friday. He had all of that and considerable more.
>
> Soon after his arrival, it seems Newcombe "tanked up." Custer is a dry town and he was thirsty Wednesday when he purchased a supply of six quart bottles of liquor and boarded a train for home.
>
> Newcombe's condition was such that the conductor ejected him from the train at Eastlake. There he was,

drunk with six bottles snugly stored away in his suitcase and not knowing where to go. Eastlakers advised him to return to Manistee and Newcombe started across the lake. He got as far as one of the timber mills by night and employees stored him away on top of the boiler to thaw out.

When Newcombe awakened Thursday, he felt himself over to ascertain if he was all there. He was—but the six bottles were gone. Still pickled, he came downtown and started to request small remittances from passersby on River Street. He was arrested by Officer Cierpka and taken to jail.

This morning Newcombe pleaded guilty before Justice Greve to a charge of being drunk and was sentenced to pay a fine of $1.00 and costs or to serve 10 days in the county jail. In default of the money he was taken back to his cell. Later he telephoned to his employer in Custer for the necessary fine, in the course of his conversation telling him that "he didn't like Manistee at all."

Soon Scottville had acquired many business enterprises. It boasted a watchmaker, blacksmith shop, creamery, restaurant, photograph gallery, two public halls, three well and windmill firms, two sales and livery stables, a tin shop, hardwood bowl mill, four dressmakers, and four resident doctors.[58] By 1887, J. N. Mack had come to town. He started a clothing and grocery store on the west side of Main Street. It was located about three fourths of the way down the street. After Mack passed away, Mrs. Mack and her son, George, continued the business until the early 1940's when they closed out the grocery part of the store and started stocking the shelves with just clothing. Later, the store became a men's clothing store and bore the name of Schulte and Thompson.

The Reader brothers had well-established businesses. George, Talcott and Fred were interested in various lines including a general line of merchandise. In 1886, Fred J. Reader established a hardware store which later became one of the largest and best known in western Michigan.[59]

C. W. McPhail established the first bank in Scottville in

the early 1890s. The bank was located about halfway down the block on Main Street. The McPhail Athletic Field on the west city limits was developed on land donated to the city by C. W. McPhail. The McPhails were noted for being very sports-minded. In major league baseball C. W. McPhail's son, Larry, was associated with the Cincinnati Reds. He also was part owner of the Brooklyn Dodgers and New York Yankees. In later years, Larry's sons were still found to be involved in major league baseball. Lee MacPhail was with the Baltimore Orioles and was president of the American League. Larry's other son, William, was vice-president for sports of the Columbia Broadcasting System.

Since the first bank was established by McPhail, there have been four buildings that have housed a bank in town. In fact, there have been two banks in Scottville. The People's State Bank and the State Savings Bank of Scottville. McPhail was affiliated with the State Savings Bank. The People's State Bank was organized in 1911.[60] In 1968, a new modern building was put up on West State Street to house the flourishing State Savings Bank of Scottville and they opened the doors of their new building in February, 1969. The People's State Bank closed their doors for the final time in the early 1930s.

A fairgrounds and racetrack were among the early forms of amusement in the early 1890s. They were established on land which was later occupied by the Stokely Van-Camp Canning Company.[61] In 1896, the last Scottville fair was held and the fair was moved to a grove of trees near Amber Town Hall just west of town. About that same period the phonograph was first coming into use, and as a sideshow attraction a person could listen in on earphones. There were no phonograph discs as yet. In later years, the county fair was relocated just east of Ludington, where it was to remain.

By 1891, a new bridge had been constructed over the Père Marquette River, south of town. The bridge was made of steel, and the stone and mortar abutments were built by John W. Griswold, a local stone mason and carpenter. Previously there had been a road set upon pilings. Logs were fitted to the top of the pilings and there was only one-way traffic over the log road and the South Bayou Bridge.[62] The new bridge certainly helped to develop the village as it made it easier for more country folk to come into town to complete their weekly shopping. The bridge was replaced by a more modern one in 1940.

During the early 1900s, some of the local businessmen started a boathouse club for summer pleasure. Their boathouses lined the banks of the Père Marquette River near the bridge and this was one of the first signs of the summer recreation and tourist possibilities in the area. Another spot of relaxation and enjoyment was the little city park which bordered the tracks south of the train depot.

By 1901, T. D. Smith had bought the business that Briggs owned, and operated it as a hardware store of his own until 1912. Briggs started a new hardware store on the east side of Main Street. From the hardware business, Smith progressed to a livery stable business, then finally to a Deering's machinery dealership. By 1903, Smith had established such an out-standing Deering machinery business that it brought him special recognition in the *Deering Farm Journal* of February, 1903. It was in this decade that the Wright Brothers of North Carolina reported that they had remained aloft in an airplane for twelve seconds.[63] In 1912, Smith and his partner, E. E. Kobe, started the Kobe and Smith Auto Company. It became the T. D. Smith Company when Kobe sold out. Smith became the first Ford car dealer in the area.[64] He and his son-in-law, Thurston Widmark, remained in the Ford car business for fifty-four years. When the first Ford cars were sent to Smith, they arrived in box cars. The bodies and wheels were put on the chassis after the cars arrived.

The first library came into being in 1899. Charles Blaine, a retired banker, donated the site and other individuals gave funds for books and the building.[65] The townfolk held box socials and other forms of entertainment to raise funds for library books.[66] This meager beginning was a far cry from what the future would hold. In 1952, a new county-city library was constructed. It was called the Mason County Library and was completed with the aid of a three-thousand-dollar grant which the library received from the Michigan State Board. In recent years, a bookmobile hatched forth from its home nest, the Mason County Library, and it can be seen each and every day as it travels about the whole county.

The charter of Scottville has been adopted by surrounding areas. It was used at the University of Michigan as a model charter for small town adoption. On February 19, 1907, Scottville became a city. Governor Warner signed a bill changing the little village into a city, and E. L. Cole became the new city's first mayor.[67] He received one hundred dollars a year for giving his services to this public office.

The year 1910 was an eventful one for Scottville. Up until then, there were only boardwalks, muddy streets, and hitching posts in the little city. By 1910, the local government had had electric lights installed and on April 4, 1910, bonds were issued for paving the city streets. Dr. W. C. Martin held the position of city mayor at that time.[68]

The local Scottville Clown Band, which is a story unto itself, was going strong by 1910. First called the Merchant's Band, its members dressed up in clown-type outfits and played for events throughout the whole state of Michigan, and have played in quite a few of the neighboring states as well. The Harvest Festival time which is held in Scottville each fall would not be the same without the clown band. Even in the band of recent years, some names have withstood the sands of time; they include Schulte, Reader, and Briggs.

The Harvest Festivals, started in the early 1900s, are remembered by all generations as a time when friendship and fun intoxicated one with the warmth, happiness, and excitement of the festival. That, too, is another story in itself.

By the summer of 1911, the local canning factory located on the old fairgrounds east of town was in full swing. The factory started out by canning peas. It was not long before they switched to canning string beans. Most of the ladies in town worked at snipping beans for the factory. They snipped the beans in their own homes. Each morning, a factory

69

representative would bring bags of beans around to the various houses and drop them off. The ladies would gather at the homes and sit on the porches, snipping beans together. They had to snip with half of a wooden clothespin, sharpened on one side, because any metal knife would rust the beans. At the close of the day, the factory man would return, pick up the beans that had been snipped and take them to the factory to be canned the next morning. In the early 1900's, the folks who worked in the W. R. Roach Canning Factory earned ten cents an hour and were given a can of beans each day to eat with their lunch. At one time, the factory was considered to be the largest string bean canning factory in the world. In 1946, Stokely Van-Camp bought the plant from the W. R. Roach Company. For a few years they even canned peaches and pears. In 1974, they canned just string beans once again.

By the end of the nineteenth century, 500 people resided in Scottville, Michigan. One of the most outstanding buildings to be built in the community was the Mason County Highway Department Building which was constructed on the east city limits in 1940. It has been known for years as one of the finest in the western part of the state.[69]

It has been said in recent years that Sweetland had become a ghost town. This certainly does not appear to be true. The village name was changed from Sweetland to Scottville, but never was the village considered to be of a "ghost town" variety.

So it was that Scottville, the little village once called Sweetland, kept growing and developing. Some of the establishments that bask in the noonday sun of the 1970s have names that still ring a familiar chord as they roll off the lips of the area folk. A few of them are Schulte and Thompson Clothing, Briggs Hardware, Scott's Sport Shop, State Savings Bank of Scottville, and Reader's Implements. Reader's just recently closed their doors for the final time. One by one, the town has bid a fond farewell to some of the old establishments. Let us hope that those who still remain will thrive right along with the rest of Scottville, Michigan — our town.

# —12—

## Courtin' Days

RUTH LOOKED at herself in the long mirror. She had heard from the other girls in town that a lady's skirt could be two inches above the ankle if there were lead weights in the hem. Ruth had a notion to talk the matter over with her mother. But what if mama did not feel that she was ready to wear such grown-up clothes? "Oh," thought Ruth, "I had better just tunk it. Mama would probably be funky about the whole thing."

Two years had passed since Irving's death, and Ruth had become more adjusted to things as they were. She was fifteen years old and had acquired more of a social life than what she had had before. There were maple syrup parties, taffy pulls, church gatherings, sleigh rides, box socials, and so many more affairs to attend. In the winter and early spring months, Ruth especially liked the "sugar parties." Folks who had made maple syrup would have a party and invite everyone in. Syrup was put on the stove until it was boiling hot. A huge basin of hard-packed snow was brought in. Then the hot syrup was drizzled on the snow. It hardened instantly and could be picked up like candy and eaten. Ruth really enjoyed the sugar parties very much.

There were the ice cream socials to go to during the hot summer months. Everyone took their turn at cranking the handle on the freezer. Ruth smiled as she thought about how the boys were so gallant and helped the "weaker" girls turn the crank. Some of the girls would act frail just to get the boys to notice them and then they would stand close by and put pieces of ice into the wooden tub and smile at the "strong" boys. Ice, in long chunks, had been cut from the Père Marquette River during the winter and placed in ice houses. The ice was imbedded in huge mounds of sawdust to preserve it for use during the summer months. As it was needed, the long chunks were hauled out, one by one, and sawed into five or ten pound pieces for the town folk to use.

By 1891, teen-aged Ruth had developed into a fine, red-haired young lady and the local swains were beginning to pay homage to her. Some of them would try to act clever for the girls. They would strut around like bantam roosters and brag about "manly" things that they had done. One would lie and the others would swear to it. Ruth would toss her red curls, turn on her heel, and walk away while the boys guffawed loudly.

There was a village water tank, fed by a windmill, just north of the main intersection in town. It was a huge, round, open wooden tank and everyone watered their cows there. Ruth would come home from school, change her clothes, and drive their four cows home from the thirteen-acre pasture which her mother owned just north of the school. The more boastful boys would wait for her there and tease just to watch her react. She would tell them, "Oh, Granny Grunt, why don't you find something better to do with your time?"

Ruth was allowed to attend parties but youngsters at that time were trained to be home when night came. If Ruth was not home by early evening, Father Loomis came for her whether the party was over or not. He would show up with a lantern in his hand and promptly escort her home. Once home, Father Loomis would lean back in his favorite chair, put his feet up on the small cricket that was nearby, close his eyes and say softly, "Everything is alright and the goose hangs high!"

One winter morning, Ruth went downstairs to find her

mother bringing a ham from the smokehouse. She had something to talk over with mama and so she reached into the cupboard and brought out the spider for her mother to brown the ham in. As they prepared breakfast, Ruth told mama about Will Jones who was one of the local boys and wanted to take her to a Christmas program. Seeing that she would not be home until quite late, she definitely had to have her mother's approval of the affair. After a short discussion, Mrs. Loomis informed her that she could go, as long as . . . She did not finish the sentence. Ruth's eyes met her mother's and she nodded her head in full understanding of what was in her mother's heart and mind.

Ruth's friend and future sister-in-law, Jessie Rozell, taught school at Lincoln River which was located quite a few miles north of town. Jessie's students were putting on a Christmas program and that was what Ruth was going to allow Jones to take her to. He arrived at the designated time, helped Ruth into his cutter, tucked the horsehair robe around her, and they started for the Lincoln River School.

The evening passed. Elhanan Loomis gathered a pile of dry wood and loaded the woodbox with it to prepare for morning. The woodbox stood near the kitchen stove. He also gathered some "chips" just in case the fire got low during the night and was hard to revive. Then, after banking the stove, he and Emma retired for the night. A few hours later, they were awakened by the entrance of a stormy, red-haired, furious "tornado" named Ruth. She was cold, shaking, and crying with indignation. It seemed that during the cutter ride home from the Christmas program, her escort had become cold himself and pulled the blanket over to protect his own body! Ruth's left leg had become frostbitten. She vowed that she surely would never allow him to escort her to anything again.

The whole affair was very mortifying to Ruth. She washed her face and hands with warm water, picked up the lamp, and headed for bed. Her mother brought a warm flatiron wrapped in a towel to put near her left leg. As Ruth blew out the light and crawled between the flannel sheets, some of her indignation cooled considerably and she chuckled to herself as she thought about one of her friends who lived quite close by. The girl had been at the Christmas program and had whispered a story to Ruth that made them both giggle.

Ruth's friend had gone to visit her aunt, who lived some few miles away. While there, she realized that she needed to empty her bladder but did not wish to travel out across a strange backyard to visit the outhouse. After bearing much discomfort, she finally informed her aunt of the problem. Being a loving relative, her aunt showed her where the "chamber-pot" was in a bedroom nearby. The girl's aunt held the lamp near the bedroom door, pointed out the white vessel, then closed the door, taking the lamp with her.

Ruth's friend felt that she knew exactly where the white container was, so she walked to that area of the dark room, turned around and lowered her "unmentionables." When she was prepared, she backed slowly down to where she "knew" the needed vessel was resting. Suddenly, a shrill cry was heard by everyone in the house. The poor girl had backed squarely into her aunt's beautiful, large cactus plant which was a little to the left of the desired place and boasted large, flat leaves with at least three inch needles!

Ruth laughed to herself as her mind pictured the whole ordeal. She rubbed her frostbitten left leg and mused half-aloud, "I suppose someday folks will laugh about this leg like I am laughing at my very own good friend's sore — ." She did not finish the sentence. Even saying it half-aloud seemed, somehow, indecent. Mama might hear and think bad thoughts concerning her morals. With a sigh of relaxation, Ruth fell into a restless sleep. Her leg was throbbing again.

In 1893, Ruth attended Ferris Institute in Big Rapids, Michigan. W. N. Ferris himself was her instructor and his brother was the school janitor, so she personally knew two members of the Ferris family. After attending Ferris Institute, Ruth came home to start her career as a "school-marm." She began teaching in 1894. Her salary was thirty dollars a month and she had to pay five dollars a month for room and board. After teaching at the Comstock School, north of Custer, Ruth signed a contract to teach at Amber Station School.

Ruth was the first person in the village of Scottville to own a bicycle. Her mother bought it for her at Reader's Hardware store and she rode it back and forth over the two-and-one-half-mile stretch to the schoolhouse where she taught. Everyone thought the bicycle was really something. It had a square seat covered with blue velvet which adjusted easily and moved as the rider moved, making it more comfortable. Not long after this, a well-worn bicycle path between Scottville and Ludington became the source of much enjoyment and pleasure to cyclists of both towns, especially the young teenaged folk.[70]

In 1894, David Falconer started to squire nineteen-year-old Ruth Bishop to many of the local social gatherings. He found that she was particularly fond of attending church-affiliated parties. Ruth's mother approved of David. He did not smoke or drink as some of the other boys did. There were boys in town who would not have been allowed to court young Ruth Bishop. They did not come up to the standards set by Emma Loomis for her red-haired daughter. No matter how old Ruth was, Emma was determined that her daughter was going to be one of good character! David was aware of Emma's feelings and intelligent enough to cater to her as well as being interested enough to want to do so. The young couple's feelings toward each other became stronger and they wanted to be together just as much as possible. By that time, David was busy with general farming and Ruth was all wrapped up in her teaching. As time passed, David Falconer and Ruth Bishop began "keepin' company" in quite a steady manner.

One night, as David was taking Ruth home from a taffy pull at the church, he seemed overly quiet and preoccupied. He looked at Ruth and studied the features of her velvet-soft face in the moonlight. Ruth said, "What are you thinking about, David?" David answered, "Ruth, in a few years I am going to settle down and make my livin' as a farmer. First, though, I just gotta see what's out west. I read about it all the time and about what is a-happenin' out there but I want to see it for myself. Ruth, I'm goin' to California to look it over. Will you wait for me 'til I come back?" Ruth told him that her teaching was going to keep her very busy and he should do whatever would make him happiest.

David spent two years working and "tramping" around California. Ruth just knew that he would find someone "nice" out there and would stay, so she would probably not be seeing him again. She wound her complete life about her teaching and decided, in her heart, that David would not be coming back to her.

One evening as Ruth helped her mother clear the supper table, she heard a soft knock at the door. Thinking it was one of mama's friends coming to visit her, she hurriedly ran to the door to make them feel welcome, as she knew her mother would wish her to do. Ruth swung open the door and her heart did a big flip-flop. There in the doorway was young David Falconer. As Ruth held out her hand to him, their eyes met. David squeezed her small hand in his large, sinewy one and Ruth knew that David Falconer had come back to her and was not going to be leaving again. He was now ready to settle down to farming and to a lifetime with Ruth.

## Ruth, the Domestic Engineer

RUTH STOOD in the middle of her bedroom and said to herself, "Sometimes we want so much we never stop to think." She wanted with all her heart to marry David Falconer and wondered if she had truly stopped long enough to think of everything. This was her wedding day! It was September 7, 1898, and David had made her blush at the party the night before when he had whispered in her ear, "Did you know that David Falconer is going to marry his old schoolmarm's little red-haired daughter?" Ruth gathered her thoughts together and called her mother in to help her fix her hair and dress for the wedding.

As Emma brushed Ruth's long, silky hair and then started to arrange the flowers she would be carrying, their eyes met. Emma cleared her throat and said in a quiet voice, "Ruth, a good wife is comparable to a delicious apple pie—not too hot to handle, and yet hot enough to warm a man to his very soul. On the other hand if she, like a pie, is too cold, she is stiff and can cool all desire for her. Every once in awhile a wife should allow her man to see enticing steam seep out through the way she walks, talks, handles him, and looks at him. This will cause her man to desire her just as he desires to savor the apple pie when he sees the steam curl and stretch aromatically out through the slits in its top crust and up through the air.

"Like the pie, a good wife should be sweet and yet hold a goodly touch of spiciness, especially when savored. A pie that is too sweet can leave one with a sickening feeling of not wanting it anymore. A sour pie can pucker up your very spine so that you shove it aside. So it is with a wife. The balance between sweetness and spiciness must be just right.

"A good wife, like the apples in a pie, must be of firm flesh and not like soggy applesauce. Yet, she must not be lumpy and hard, but her body should have soft form that melts in her husband's arms as the slices of apples melt in one's mouth. When savored, a wife's spirit should be warm and flow toward her husband as the juice from the apple pie flows out slightly when a piece is removed to savor. Just as a wife sees to it that her husband's desire for a good apple pie is fulfilled, so should she see to it that he enjoys a good wife!"

Emma turned toward the door. Mother and daughter both had tears of understanding and emotion swimming in their eyes. Ruth answered, "Mama, I shall never forget what you have told me, nor shall I ever forget how close we have been to each other." There was a soft knock on the door and Emma Loomis left so that she would be in the parlor when her daughter arrived from upstairs.

A bubbly Lenna Wheeler, Ruth's bridesmaid, entered the room. She looked at Ruth and breathed, "Oh, how radiant you look! David's eyes will fall right out when he sees you!" Ruth laughed, then asked if very many people were downstairs. After all, she and her mother had invited and prepared for fifty-four people in all. Lenna said that everyone had arrived and that the lower floor of the house was truly packed with bodies! Ruth was so thankful that her mother had prepared plenty of cake and coffee. Emma Loomis had made four kinds of cake in all. She had made extra of all four kinds and had put a tiny piece of each one in small blue boxes tied with ribbons and had placed them by the front door so that each guest would have a memento to take home with them.

Ruth searched the top of her dresser for her lace-edged handkerchief and asked if Reverend McDonald had arrived.

Lenna said that he had. Reverend A. P. McDonald was the Baptist minister in Ludington and was coming over especially for the wedding as mama had requested him to do. Lenna looked at Ruth and said with a laugh, "And David is here too! He is here with all of his relatives and even his grandmother from Scotland! It is going to be a wonderful wedding. James, David's brother, is ready to be his best man so now all they need is you, Ruth!" Ruth smiled at Lenna and they turned to go downstairs. When Ruth reached the bottom of the steps, she saw the familiar faces of all of their friends as they smiled at her. C. D. Coddington was there, as was George Reader and her stepsister, Via Loomis. The other Reader brothers and their families had come. So had the Schultes, the Niels, and so many others.

David and Ruth were married in one corner of the parlor in her mother's home. He built a new house on a tract of land just northeast of Scottville and they settled there to raise cattle, vegetables, and seven healthy, lively children. During her career as a domestic engineer, Ruth developed many talents she was unaware that she possessed. Besides giving birth to seven children within seventeen "busy" years, she developed her ability to milk cows, raise a garden, cook for threshers, can vegetables, and other things too numerous to mention. Her children were quite close in age as one can see by noticing their years of birth:

                    1902 — Emma
                    1905 — Jesse
                    1907 — Wallace
                    1910 — Ruth
                    1912 — David
                    1914 — Grace
                    1919 — Lawrence

Yes, she felt that they were very busy years, but years full of happiness and many memories.

Besides managing her home and family, Ruth was always

quite busy with social events in Scottville. By then the new library had been constructed. David and Ruth both took an active part in all of the money-raising events to help purchase library books. They realized that not only would the town benefit; their own children would glean from it as they grew older and attended school. Ruth and David were anxious for their children to have the best education that they were capable of achieving and they wanted them to also have a taste of the cultural niceties of life. They felt that things like the library would help gain their desires for them.

The years passed and Ruth was kept busy with her home and family. By the year 1910, three of her seven children were on earth requiring her attention and her daughter, Ruth, was born. They had moved from the north road farm to another one on State Road which proved to be U. S. 10, between Scottville and Custer. David had been selling milk to some of the families in town. Soon more milk was required than his cows were able to produce and he bought milk and cream from his neighbors, bottled it, and sold it to his customers. Thus, the Falconer Dairy came into being. They had a horse-drawn, narrow, box-type wagon that they used to pick the milk up from the farmers. Then they took it to their own farm to be bottled.

Two men worked for them as hired hands. One did nothing but wash bottles and care for the milk. The other broke ice and helped with the making of ice cream. At one time, they furnished all of the milk that was being delivered to Epworth Heights, near Ludington. At the same time, they made at least twenty-five gallons of ice cream each Saturday to deliver to Claveau's Ice Cream Parlor in Scottville and to Epworth. This would last just through Sunday of each week. Having the dairy proved at times to be a trial. Some women on the route wanted regular milk, some wanted fresh cow milk for their babies, and some wanted only heifer milk. Each customer's bottles had to be marked and kept separate which proved to be, as Ruth called it, "a caution." David Falconer told everyone that he thought he had really married a dairy maid.

One Sunday morning, Ruth accompanied David on his milk route. They were collecting milk from the neighbors to take back to their place and bottle it for town. As the horses walked along, Ruth and David enjoyed the bright sunshine and listened to the birds that were singing from the treetops. They were at peace with the world and happy just to be in each other's company. Suddenly, an object they had never seen before came over the hill and right toward them. The horses bolted, as the contraption sounded just like a huge threshing machine! Ruth knew that it must be one of those new-fangled automobiles, but it did not look like the touring cars that she had seen pictures of. It was a fire-engine red, little pick-up runabout. It stopped nearby and after David settled the horses, they looked to see who was driving the contraption. Their good friend Charlie Neer hopped out of it and came toward them. He had a big, wide grin on his face because he held the distinction of being one of the first in Scottville to own a car.

Ruth sat down after lunch and picked up the newspaper. She wanted to read it while she drank a second cup of coffee. The date at the top of the paper read, "Monday, April 15, 1918." The front page of the paper was covered with articles concerning World War I which was in progress. Ruth's mind wandered back to the "hanging" that had taken place in Scottville during the war. The Andre Hotel had burned down long before and all there was left on the northeast corner of the main crossroads in town was a large hole in the ground. Patriotism ran high among all ages in town and there had been a huge bonfire built at one corner of the hole. Then, along with much shouting, speech-making, and patriotic singing, they had hung the German Kaiser in effigy!

Ruth thought about some of the war stories that folks were telling in town. Whenever she or David went in after supplies, they heard them. Two days earlier, David had heard about the two Palmer boys, nephews of David and Anna Reinoehl who lived south of town. Ben Palmer was with some soldiers who were being moved out of the front line trenches for rest. As they marched out, Ben met his brother, Otto, who

81

was one of the replacements. Ben forgot all about the rest that he so badly needed. He stepped out of line, fell in step with his brother, and marched right back in to fight at Otto's side.

Ruth's family did not feel the effects of the war as much as the townfolk did. After all, they raised their own meat, vegetables, and fruits. There was always plenty of milk, butter, and hickory-smoked hams in the cool milkhouse. On the shelves in the pantry were rows and rows of glass jars filled with string beans, corn, and other vegetables. David and Ruth had been very busy on the farm, but their youngsters were happy and had full "tummys."

During 1929 and 1930, Herbert C. Hoover was president of the United States of America. Depression days, or "Hoover Days" as they were called by many, were sadly felt in the city of Scottville as well as over the rest of the nation. During the Crash of '29 it was difficult for the town folks to make a decent living, and many local people used up or lost all of their life savings. Stock prices fell to fifty per cent of what they had been only a few weeks before.[71] A lot of the banks in the area, as well as nationwide, were closing their doors and folks were not able to get their savings out. This did not happen with The State Savings Bank of Scottville. People were given time to collect on loans and the bank was only closed temporarily. A national bank holiday was called and The State Savings Bank of Scottville was closed between Lincoln's and Washington's birthdays, but reopened again right after that.

Ruth helped the local churches as many farm wives did. Their own families were gleaning from the soil and did not go hungry. Ruth would fill a cardboard box with goodies from her own larder and take it in for the church to give to a needy family. Never a Sunday went by but what Ruth had extra folks in for dinner. Usually it was a "town family," one that might have gone without if she had not asked them to dine with her family. It got to the point that "Sunday company" for dinner was the usual and expected thing.

William Rohrmoser, a local carpenter, was out of work as

no one could possibly be interested in doing any building during "Hoover Days." He was a good example of what depression days were like for Scottville people. After many days of trying desperately to find work, he finally obtained the position of Scottville City Marshal. The wages offered were eighty dollars per month, which sounded quite good for depression wages! After starting his job as City Marshal, Rohrmoser found that the city was able to pay eighty dollars per month because he was also considered to be the water commissioner, street commissioner, WPA manager, city carpenter, city cement worker, relief manager, water tank manager, water bill collector, and head of the local vigilantes. In fact, Rohrmoser was the instigator in the making out of bills for water that the residents used. It was also at this time that the city sewers were put in under the guidance of Rohrmoser and the WPA workers. Even though Rohrmoser was over-worked, he was one of the few fortunate ones in town that had employment during the depression years.

Ruth and David left the farm and moved into Emma Loomis' house in 1941, during World War II. Ruth's mother had passed away in 1915 and she had rented her mother's house out to others since then. As she and David grew older, the farm and dairy began to be too much for them to handle. They moved the dairy to a building directly across the street from her mother's home and David went on with the dairy business. He bought milk from the farmers and brought it to town to bottle. It was just a small dairy, but enough to keep him occupied. World War II did not cause their family too much heartache. Only Lawrence, their youngest son, had to go into the service and he returned safely. They were affected, as everyone else, by food and gas rationing, but with the dairy they always seemed to have enough and did not go without. Life was full of contentment for them. Each evening, Ruth and David would sit on their front porch and listen to the robins singing in the maple trees by the dairy. They were very, very happy.

# —14—

# And So, Tomorrow

ONE EVENING, in 1947, Ruth and David Falconer returned from attending a neighborhood party. It was after midnight and they were quite tired. As they prepared for bed, David informed Ruth that his side was giving him quite a bit of pain. A worried look crossed Ruth's face. David had a hernia that he was forced to "baby" along, and had been doing so for sixteen years. He wore a brace for it each and every day. There were even times when he wore it to bed to alleviate pain. In fact, he had already undergone surgery for it once before. Toward morning, David roused Ruth and told her that the pain was more than he could bear. He was rushed by ambulance to the hospital where he was given medication to deaden the pain. By morning, the hospital had contacted his doctor and surgery was definitely necessary. David seemed to sense that he would not live long. As they wheeled him into the operating room, he reached out his hand to Ruth and said, "Please, I want my four sons and two sons-in-law to carry me to my grave." The doctor found that the hernia had burst and David passed away that afternoon. Ruth fulfilled his wish. His four sons and two sons-in-law gently carried him to his grave and he was buried at Scottville's Brookside Cemetery near Ruth's mother.

The next few months were difficult ones for Ruth. She knew that she would never get over David's death. She would, instead, have to adjust and learn to live with it! Almost thirty years later, when this book was written, she still has not gotten over his death but has learned to accept it. She stated to the author, "One never does get over something like that when you love someone so terribly much." Since David's death, she has slept every single night with his watch tucked under her pillow. It is a large railroad pocket watch, and its loud ticking seems to help her feel closer to David.

Six months after David's death, she lost one of her sons-in-law. He experienced an unexpected heart attack while in a boat, fell out, and drowned. Ruth picked up the pieces of her life and, with the help of her seven children, she "carried on." Two of her children lived in other parts of Michigan. The other five lived right in Scottville. All seven are still living and go home to see their mother very, very often. Ruth still writes to her adopted sister, Via, who is in a rest home in another part of Michigan.

The author asked Ruth how she felt about Scottville after all the years that she has lived in the city. She answered, "Scottville is still quite a lively, little burg. It is trying desperately to be quite modern. There are many, many improvements throughout the whole town. I feel it is rightly known as 'The Busiest Little City in Michigan.' When you see the businessmen of today taking part so willingly in such things as the yearly chicken barbecue, then you know that they all still care. Yes, Scottville looks wonderful to me. I would not feel at home in any other place. I have enjoyed it for ninety some years and have really grown up with my home town."

Ruth will, some day, be starting her "tour of duty" in Heaven. She is prepared for it. There is a space for her at Brookside Cemetery right between her husband and her mother. This is very fitting. They were the two people who had the most influence over her life. She loved them dearly, and always will. But until that "some day" comes, Ruth goes to bed each night and prays, "Dear Lord, if you see fit to take me tonight, I am ready. But, if you need me here yet, I am ready for that too." The author and all of Scottville salute Ruth. She is truly the town's leading lady. Scottville is proud of her.

The city can well be proud of its own growth also. It has been known far and wide by the slogan "The Busiest Little City in Michigan." Automobiles, fine paved streets, beautiful homes, civic pride in our surroundings, an up-to-date movie theater, fine schools, a high school band and athletic teams with great promise, the noted Scottville Clown Band, a good athletic field, and many organizations all denote the community's progress. There are now over fifteen hundred residents who call Scottville home.[72]

There are so many other points of interest concerning Scottville and the author is finding it very frustrating to have to close the door on them and draw this narrative to an end. There is the Scottville River Park that was created from the dreams and labors of J. Ralph Reeds and some of the town fathers. There are all the pioneer families; their sorrows and joys; their successes and failures. If one were to stand on the very spot where Reader and Scott once flipped a coin to name the town, one could cast his eyes to the north, south, east, or west and see where the pioneers have left their mark on the little city called Scottville. One would also be able to observe the descendants of those same pioneers as they scurry here and there; making still more history for tomorrow. Yes, if one were to stand near the main intersection of town and look around, he would see that tomorrow's history is shouting to be made while today's history is but a whisper.

And so, tomorrow! The author, Ruth, and all of the other residents of Scottville must now turn our countenances toward our own personal tomorrows, whatever they might bring. But, still, it is with a little touch of sadness, sadness over having to leave this story of Scottville only half told, that makes the author repeat again, "How pleasant! How truly pleasant it is to look back; back to frontier days!"

Ruth Falconer, the Matriarch of Scottville.
Picture taken on her 97th birthday, 1973.

Asa Bishop, Ruth's father. Picture copied
from a tintype—courtesy of Ruth Falconer.

Ruth Bishop, age three, sitting on Grandpa's couch.
Picture copied from a tintype—courtesy of Ruth Falconer

Baby Ruth Bishop, aged one year.
Picture copied from a tintype—courtesy of Ruth Falconer

Shopping in busy little Scottville, Michigan, 1910.
(Looking north from the railroad tracks.) Original
picture in possession of George Mack, Scottville,
Michigan

A modern Scottville, Michigan.
Looking south from stoplight. Original picture in
possession of Russ Miller, Ludington, Michigan.

Ruth Bishop, age five years, and her mother on her mother's wedding day. Picture copied from a tintype—courtesy of Ruth Falconer.

Ruth, nine years old, and her family.
Picture courtesy of Ruth Falconer

Scottville Methodist Church, built in 1890.
Original picture in possession of author.

Scottville United Methodist Church, 1974.
Original picture in possession of author.

Scottville Clown Band (Merchant's Band), 1910.
Original picture in possession of Raymond Schulte,
Scottville, Michigan.

Harvest Festival Days, 1910.
Original picture in possession of George Mack,
Scottville, Michigan.

David and Ruth Falconer in 1943, married 45 years.
Picture courtesy of Ruth Falconer.

David Falconer and Ruth Bishop on their wedding
day, September 7, 1898.
Picture courtesy of Ruth Falconer.

One of Scottville's girls' basketball teams.
Flossie Reader Mack is found on the extreme left.
Picture courtesy of George Mack, Scottville,
Michigan.

Ruth Falconer, 96 years old, with the wax fruit that
her mother made during Civil War days.
Picture courtesy Ludington Daily News, Ludington,
Michigan

# NOTES

1. Author unknown, *History of Manistee, Mason, and Oceana Counties, Chicago:* H. R. Pace and Co., 1882, p. 77.
2. *Ibid.*, p. 81.
3. *Ibid.*, p. 8.
4. O. C., Crandall, "The Riverman's Last Farewell," Copyright 1932, p. 8.
5. Henry F. Graff, *The Free and the Brave,* Chicago: Rand McNally and Co., 1967, p. 418.
6. F. Clever Bald, *Michigan in Four Centuries*, New York: Harper and Row, 1954, p. 229.
7. Emma E. Barclay, "Scottville's History Recalled by Many," *Ludington Daily News,* February 22, 1955, p. 5, column 3.
8. *Ibid.*
9. *History of Manistee, Mason, and Oceana Counties,* Chicago: p. 53.
10. *Ibid.*, p. 12.
11. Lillian M., Schulte, "Memories of Scottville," *Mason County Press,* January 27, 1955, p. 5, column 1.
12. Lillian M., Schulte, "History of City Traced from 1860," *Ludington Daily News,* June 24, 1952, Section 3, p. 2, column 1.
13. Emma E., Barclay, "Scottville's History Recalled by Many," *Ludington Daily News,* February 22, 1955, p. 5, column 3.
14. *Ibid.*
15. "History of Scottville," *Ludington Daily News,* May 6, 1944, p. 5, column 1.
16. Emma E. Barclay, "Scottville's History Recalled by Many," *Ludington Daily News.*
17. Lillian M. Schulte, "Memories of Scottville," *Mason County Press.*
18. "History of Scottville," *Ludington Daily News.*

19. Schulte, "Memories of Scottville," *Mason County Press.*
20. Ferris E. Lewis, *Michigan Yesterday and Today,* Michigan: Hillsdale Educational Publishers, Inc., 1969, p. 234.
21. Barclay, "Scottville's History Recalled by Many," *Ludington Daily News.*
22. "History of Scottville," *Ludington Daily News,* May 6, 1944.
23. *Ibid.*
24. Charles Anderson, "City Has an Interesting History," *Mason County Press,* September 24, 1959.
25. "Scott and Crowley Build New Store," *Mason County Record,* December 12, 1879.
26. "History of Scottville," *Ludington Daily News,* May 6, 1944.
27. Barclay, "Scottville's History Recalled by Many," *Ludington Daily News.*
28. Henry F. Graff, *The Free and the Brave,* p. 491.
29. Barclay, "Scottville's History Recalled by Many," *Ludington Daily News.*
30. *Ibid.*
31. "Brief History of Schools of Scottville," *Scottville Enterprise,* March 15, 1917.
32. "History of Scottville," *Ludington Daily News,* May 6, 1944.
33. "Brief History of Schools of Scottville, *Scottville Enterprise.* March 15, 1917.
34. *Ibid.,* page 1, column 2.
35. *Ibid.*
36. "Steady Progress Marks History of Scottville School Since 1877," *Mason County Enterprise,* April 26, 1928.
37. "Faculty List Is Announced," *Mason County Press,* September 1, 1955, p. 3, column 1.
38. "To Hold School Meeting Monday," *Mason County Press,* June 13, 1955.
39. "Thousands Will Return to Classes After Summer Holiday," *Mason County Press,* August 30, 1956.

40. "Sunday, May 7 is Arnold Carlson Day," *Mason County Press*, May 4, 1967, column 5.
41. Barclay, "Scottville's History Recalled by Many," *Ludington Daily News.*
42. Charles Anderson, "City Has an Interesting History," *Mason County Press.*
43. Barclay, "Scottville's History Recalled by Many," *Ludington Daily News.*
44. Charles Anderson, "City Has an Interesting History," *Mason County Press.*
45. Schulte, "History of City Traced from 1860," *Ludington Daily News.*
46. Barclay, "Scottville's History Recalled by Many," *Ludington Daily News.*
47. "First Frame House Built in Scottville Is Still Standing," *Ludington Daily News,* June 22, 1948, p. 4, column 1.
48. Henry F. Graff, *The Free and the Brave,* p. 488, column 1.
49. Schulte, "History of City Traced From 1860," *Ludington Daily News.*
50. *Ibid.*
51. J. Ralph Reeds, "Interesting History of Post Office in City of Scottville," *Mason County Press,* October 8, 1959, p. 8, column 4.
52. J. Ralph Reeds, "Postmaster Tells of First Post Office in Scottville," *Ludington Daily News,* October 8, 1959, p. 6, column 3.
53. Orin Kaye, Jr., " 'Horse and Buggy' Rural Mail Delivery Offers Sharp Contrast to New Highway Postal Service," *Muskegon Chronicle,* November 9, 1949, p. 24, column 1.
54. J. Ralph Reeds, "Interesting History of Post Office in City of Scottville," *Mason County Press.*
55. Henry F. Graff, *The Free and the Brave,* p. 491, column 2.
56. Schulte, "History of City Traced From 1860," *Ludington Daily News.*
57. *Ibid.*

58. *Ibid.*
59. "History of Scottville," *Ludington Daily News.*
60. "Peoples' State Bank Has Increased Its Deposits," *Scottville Enterprise,* March 15, 1917, p. 1, column 4.
61. Schulte, "History of City Traced From 1860," *Ludington Daily News.*
62. J. P. Griswold, "Once Upon a Time," *Mason County Press,* August 2, 1973, p. 4, column 2.
63. Henry F. Graff, *The Free and the Brave,* p. 605, column 2.
64. Schulte, "History of City Traced from 1860," *Ludington Daily News,* June 24, 1952, Section 3, p. 2, column 2.
65. *Ibid.,* Section 4, p. 4, column 2.
66. Ruth Van Der Molen, "History of Scottville Library," *Mason County Press,* October 8, 1959, p. 5, column 1.
67. Charles Anderson, "City Has an Interesting History," *Mason County Press.*
68. "History of Scottville," *Ludington Daily News.*
69. Emma E. Barclay, "First Frame House Built in Scottville Is Still Standing," *Ludington Daily News,* June 22, 1948, p. 4, column 2.
70. "History of Scottville," *Ludington Daily News.*
71. Henry F. Graff, *The Free and the Brave,* p. 627, column 1.
72. Schulte, "History of City Traced From 1860," *Ludington Daily News.*

# BIBLIOGRAPHY

## Books

1. Author Unknown, *History of Manistee, Mason, and Oceana Counties,* Chicago: H. R. Pace and Co., 1882.
2. Bald, F. Clever, *Michigan in Four Centuries,* New York: Harper and Row, 1954.
3. Graff, Henry F., *The Free and the Brave,* Chicago: Rand McNally and Co., 1967.
4. Lewis, Ferris E., *Michigan Yesterday and Today,* Michigan: Hillsdale Educational Publishers, Inc., 1969.

## Newspaper Articles

1. Schulte, Lillian M.    "Memories of Scottville," *Mason County Press,* January 27, 1955.
2. "To Hold School Meeting Monday," *Mason County Press,* June 13, 1955.
3. "Faculty List Is Announced," *Mason County Press,* September 1, 1955.
4. "Thousands Will Return to Classes After Summer Holiday," *Mason County Press,* August 30, 1956.
5. Anderson, Charles, "City Has an Interesting History," *Mason County Press,* September 24, 1959.
6. Reeds, J. Ralph, "Interesting History of Post Office in City of Scottville," *Mason County Press,* October 8, 1959.
7. Van Der Molen, Ruth, "History of Scottville Library," *Mason County Press,* October 8, 1959.
8. "Sunday, May 7 is Arnold Carlson Day," *Mason County Press,* May 4, 1967.
9. Griswold, J. P., "Once Upon a Time," *Mason County Press,* August 2, 1973.
10. "History of Scottville," *Ludington Daily News,* May 6, 1944.

11. "First Frame House Built in Scottville Is Still Standing," *Ludington Daily News,* June 22, 1948.
12. Schulte, Lillian M., "History of City Traced From 1860," *Ludington Daily News,* June 24, 1952.
13. Barclay, Emma E., "Scottville's History Recalled by Many," *Ludington Daily News,* February 22, 1955.
14. Reeds, J. Ralph, "Postmaster Tells of First Post Office in Scottville," *Ludington Daily News,* October 8, 1959.
15. "Brief History of Schools of Scottville," *Scottville Enterprise,* March 15, 1917.
16. "Steady Progress Marks History of Scottville's School Since 1877," *Mason County Enterprise,* April 26, 1928.
17. "Scott and Crowley Build New Store," *Mason County Record,* December 12, 1879.
18. Kaye, Orin, Jr., " 'Horse and Buggy' Rural Mail Delivery Offers Sharp Contrast to New Highway Postal Service," *Muskegon Chronicle,* November 9, 1949.

*Manuscripts*

1. Crandall, O.C., *The Riverman's Last Farewell,* Copyright 1932.
2. Newkirk, O. J. Jr., *Ruth, Scottville's Leading Lady.*